The
Baby Boom

The
Baby Boom

Other books in the Turning Points series:

Turning Points

IN WORLD HISTORY

The
Baby Boom

Stuart A. Kallen, *Book Editor*

Daniel Leone, *President*
Bonnie Szumski, *Publisher*
Scott Barbour, *Managing Editor*

Greenhaven Press, Inc., San Diego, California

Every effort has been made to trace the owners of copyrighted material. The articles in this volume may have been edited for content, length, and/or reading level. The titles have been changed to enhance the editorial purpose.

Library of Congress Cataloging-in-Publication Data

The baby boom / Stuart A. Kallen, book editor.
  p. cm. — (Turning points in world history)
  Includes bibliographical references and index.
  ISBN 0-7377-0925-1 (lib. bdg. : alk. paper)
  ISBN 0-7377-0924-3 (pbk. : alk. paper)
  1. Baby boom generation—United States. 2. United States—
Social conditions—20th century. I. Kallen, Stuart A., 1955–
II. Series.
HN59 .B23 2002
306'.0904—dc21   2001037224
                                                 CIP

Cover photo: SuperStock
Library of Congress: 16, 19, 24, 26, 42, 65, 71, 115

© 2002 by Greenhaven Press, Inc.
10911 Technology Place, San Diego, CA 92127

Printed in the U.S.A.

Contents

Chapter 5: Growing Old

Foreword

Certain past events stand out as pivotal, as having effects and outcomes that change the course of history. These events are often referred to as turning points. Historian Louis L. Snyder provides this useful definition:

> A turning point in history is an event, happening, or stage which thrusts the course of historical development into a different direction. By definition a turning point is a great event, but it is even more—a great event with the explosive impact of altering the trend of man's life on the planet.

History's turning points have taken many forms. Some were single, brief, and shattering events with immediate and obvious impact. The invasion of Britain by William the Conqueror in 1066, for example, swiftly transformed that land's political and social institutions and paved the way for the rise of the modern English nation. By contrast, other single events were deemed of minor significance when they occurred, only later recognized as turning points. The assassination of a little-known European nobleman, Archduke Franz Ferdinand, on June 28, 1914, in the Bosnian town of Sarajevo was such an event; only after it touched off a chain reaction of political-military crises that escalated into the global conflict known as World War I did the murder's true significance become evident.

Other crucial turning points occurred not in terms of a few hours, days, months, or even years, but instead as evolutionary developments spanning decades or even centuries. One of the most pivotal turning points in human history, for instance—the development of agriculture, which replaced nomadic hunter-gatherer societies with more permanent settlements—occurred over the course of many generations. Still other great turning points were neither events nor developments, but rather revolutionary new inventions and innovations that significantly altered social customs and ideas, military tactics, home life, the spread of knowledge, and the human condition in general. The developments of writing, gunpowder, the printing press, antibiotics, the electric light, atomic energy, television, and the computer, the last two of which have recently ushered in the world-altering information age, represent only some of these innovative turning points.

Each anthology in the Greenhaven Turning Points in World History series presents a group of essays chosen for their accessibility. The anthology's structure also enhances this accessibility. First, an introductory essay provides a general overview of the principal events and figures involved, placing the topic in its historical context. The essays that follow explore various aspects in more detail, some targeting political trends and consequences, others social, literary, cultural, and/or technological ramifications, and still others pivotal leaders and other influential figures. To aid the reader in choosing the material of immediate interest or need, each essay is introduced by a concise summary of the contributing writer's main themes and insights.

In addition, each volume contains extensive research tools, including a collection of excerpts from primary source documents pertaining to the historical events and figures under discussion. In the anthology on the French Revolution, for example, readers can examine the works of Rousseau, Voltaire, and other writers and thinkers whose championing of human rights helped fuel the French people's growing desire for liberty; the French *Declaration of the Rights of Man and Citizen*, presented to King Louis XVI by the French National Assembly on October 2, 1789; and eyewitness accounts of the attack on the royal palace and the horrors of the Reign of Terror. To guide students interested in pursuing further research on the subject, each volume features an extensive bibliography, which for easy access has been divided into separate sections by topic. Finally, a comprehensive index allows readers to scan and locate content efficiently. Each of the anthologies in the Greenhaven Turning Points in World History series provides students with a complete, detailed, and enlightening examination of a crucial historical watershed.

Introduction: The Influences of a Generation

More than 75 million American men and women are classified as baby boomers. The term refers to a generation born at a time when the nation's birth rate was at a record high. Researchers place the boom between 1946 and 1964, but a baby "boomlet" began as early as 1942 as couples had children before men went off to fight World War II. Regardless of their birth date relative to others in this range, the baby boomers represent a huge demographic "bubble" that has been moving through society for decades. As William Sterling and Stephen Waite describe it in *Boomernomics:*

> Demographers have used the image of a pig slowly passing through the body of a python to describe the massive displacement created by baby boomers as they have passed through different stages of life. . . . The boomer generation is huge compared to both the preceding generation and the following generation.[1]

The baby boom generation is unique in history for other reasons as well. Theirs was a generation whose parents lived through the Great Depression and World War II and were therefore influenced by the ideals fostered during these events. It was also a generation that predominantly grew up in the newly created suburbs of major cities. Economic prosperity was a new phenomenon generated on the heels of a booming wartime economy, and boomers were the first generation treated to its luxuries, including the all-important television set. Not all of these aspects of the postwar society were universal, but all were commonplace nonetheless. Their influences on the boomers held the generation together, giving them shared points of reference and cultural unity that seemed to bond even those boomers who did not always enjoy the advantages of their neighbors.

The Generations Before

By comparing the culture of the baby boom generation with that of their parents and grandparents, it is easy to see why boomers were drastically different from those who came before them. While the baby boomers experienced a period of extended adolescence that lasted until their late twenties, most of their parents and grandparents had full-time jobs by the time they were fifteen or sixteen years of age. Farm children worked with their parents in fields, city children labored in factories or became apprentices to craftsmen. Upper-class boys and girls might have attended college, but most prewar Americans began working before they turned eighteen, and many never stopped until they died.

As Kenneth Keniston writes in *Young Radicals: Notes on Committed Youth*, the parents of the baby boomers were raised to follow the rules that "emphasized respect, the control of impulse, obedience to authority, and the traditional . . . values of hard work, deferred gratification, and self-restraint."[2]

While they were taught to work hard and save as the means to success, the parents of the baby boomers grew up in the worst of times. Many were born around 1920 and grew up in the prosperous times of the Roaring Twenties. But in 1929, the U.S. economy crashed, ushering in the worst economic depression in history. Between 1930 and 1933, stocks of U.S. companies lost 80 percent of their value. Eleven thousand banks failed, the jobless rate grew to more than 25 percent, and millions of people experienced hunger, homelessness, and general despair. The depression ended with the onset of World War II in Europe in 1939, and the American economy was boosted by wartime industrial expansion.

Almost to a man, the fathers of the earliest baby boomers served in the military during World War II. It was a time when everyone from janitors to movie stars was expected to fight; over 50 million men registered for the draft and more than 12 million were serving in the military at any given time between 1940 and 1945.

After the war, with Europe and Asia in ruin, the United States emerged as the strongest and wealthiest nation on Earth, a world superpower for the first time. To the young men and women who had lived through the hard times of the depression, and then the horrors of World War II, it was a time to go to school, get a secure job, and live the American Dream. Above all, most promised themselves that their children would never experience the poverty, fear, and uncertainty that they had recently put behind them.

As the 1950s dawned, the social values in the United States squarely emphasized marriage, children, and family. Men and women began to marry at an earlier age, on average twenty-two for men and nineteen for women. The divorce rate, which had risen slowly from the 1920s, leveled off at 10 percent. Divorce was stigmatized and considered socially unacceptable.

Before the fifties, due to housing shortages and economic hard times, children usually grew up in households that included their grandparents, aunts, uncles, and other extended family members. But in the fifties, suburban "nuclear families" predominated, consisting of mother, father, and children only. These families did almost everything together. They went to church, took vacations, watched ballgames, worked in the yard, washed the car and watched a lot of television. And they multiplied. Between 1946 and 1964, over 75 million children were born—more than 4 million a year after the mid-1950s. (In 1957, a baby was born every seven seconds in America.) This "baby boom" formed a huge demographic bulge that influenced everything from the sale of diapers and cars to the popularity of rock and roll.

Suburbs and Television

This population boom quickly changed the face of America, filling hospital maternity wards and boosting the sales of diapers and baby food to unprecedented levels. More people employed in a growing economy with growing families needed new homes, and suburban housing was erected at a record pace. By the late 1950s, more than 60 million people—nearly one-third of all Americans—had moved to brand-new suburbs that had been built in little more than a decade.

Every suburban living room had a television set, and baby boomers were the first generation to be raised on a steady diet of TV situation comedies, or sitcoms, variety shows, westerns, and dramas. Although television was invented in the late 1930s, in 1946 only seven thousand TV sets existed in the United States. By 1950, 4.4 million families were tuning in to the wonders of television. By 1956, people in the United States were buying TV sets at the rate of twenty thousand a day. In 1960, Americans owned 50 million televisions and 90 percent of homes had at least one TV.

Sales of televisions indirectly boosted sales of other items and created unexpected new markets. In 1955 alone, for example, Americans bought 4 million new refrigerators so they could store another new invention—frozen TV dinners. During the baby boom era, the traditional family sit-down dinner was replaced by people consuming convenience foods from aluminum trays in front of the TV. Ironically, all the family-oriented sitcoms showed mothers, fathers, and children traditionally gathered for meals around a large dining room table.

Raised on Rock

While TV was the centerpiece of fifties family life, another, louder, more insistent beat was central to the lives of millions of teens. Rock and roll music painted a wild rainbow of color across a conformist suburban landscape where most people looked alike, dressed alike, and to some extent thought alike.

In the early 1950s, the smoky rhythm and blues (R&B) emanating from African American radio stations was called "boogie-woogie" or "race music." But white teens from the suburbs began buying large numbers of R&B records. In 1951 Cleveland disc jockey Alan Freed began to play some of the hot new records on *The Moondog Show*. The radio signal was so strong that it skipped across the stratosphere to a vast area of the Midwest. Teenagers from rural towns, big cities, and nearby suburbs could tune in Freed spinning records, chattering wildly, and beating on a Cleveland phone book with a drumstick. Freed stuck to the black roots of rock and helped make stars of such artists as Fats Domino, Johnny Ace, Johnny Otis, the Drifters, the Platters, and the Moonglows.

White musicians began to capitalize on the rock explosion

in the spring of 1955, when MGM released the movie *The Blackboard Jungle* about a high school teacher confronted by violent students. The opening credits appeared to the soundtrack of "Rock Around the Clock" by Bill Haley and the Comets. Teenaged theater patrons energized by the tune actually rioted in some cities. Sales were bolstered by controversy and the record quickly sold more than a million copies—a huge number by fifties standards.

By the summer of 1955, black rock artists were also en-

With his unique voice and personal appeal, Elvis Presley did more to advance rock and roll than any other musician of his time.

joying unprecedented success. Chuck Berry's "Maybellene" was a number-one hit, closely followed by Little Richard's "Tutti Frutti." Black music was so popular, in fact, that record producer Sam Phillips said, "If I could find a white man with a Negro sound, I could make billions of dollars."[3] Very soon, Phillips found his man—a Tennessee youth named Elvis Presley.

Singer–guitar player Presley was tough and sensual with greased-back hair and a leather jacket, and his emotion-charged "Heartbreak Hotel" shot to the top of the *Billboard* magazine best-seller charts on April 21, 1956. Elvis followed "Heartbreak Hotel" with a string of hits that made him a household name. For fifty-five of the next one hundred weeks, Elvis would have the best-selling records in America with "Hound Dog," "Don't Be Cruel," "All Shook Up," "Love Me Tender," and others. Elvis influenced hundreds of thousands of kids to pick up guitars and learn to sing and play. Guitar sales across the country in 1950 were about 228,000; by 1959 that number had jumped to 400,000.

The influence of rock music on the baby boomers cannot be underestimated. While musical fads had come and gone in earlier decades, the rebellious sounds of rock and roll have had a profound and lasting impact on society. Rock allowed baby boomers to ignore the most repressive aspects of fifties society, and in the 1960s rock music became the prime medium of protest and social commentary, reaching nearly every segment of society in nearly every corner of the globe. Boomers are quick to credit their tastes for their musical contribution to culture. As Bruce Pollock writes in *Hipper than Our Kids:*

> I believe in my inmost heart that if we were not the ones who actually invented rock & roll, we were certainly the ones who bought it, adopted it, adapted it, embraced it—did everything short of wearing it out like an old sneaker. . . . [After Elvis Presley appeared on the *Ed Sullivan Show* in 1956 we were] a sub-teen generation in pajamas . . . shell-shocked straight into puberty overnight. . . . [We] carved out of the available sources a unique all-purpose amalgam that would stand until the millennium and . . . beyond, managing at the same time to extend our own pubescence well into middle-age![4]

Dark Side of the Fifties

While the happy teenager dancing around the living room to Elvis Presley remains a lasting image of the fifties, the era also held a dark side. After World War II, the Communist-led Soviet Union embarked on a crash program to develop its own nuclear weapons and challenge the superpower status of the United States. As the two powers battled for world domination they began to build and test hydrogen bombs with one hundred times the destructive power of the atom bombs dropped on Japan. The military stalemate between the competing superpowers was known as the cold war. Each nation stockpiled thousands of weapons that could destroy the entire planet within minutes. There was an ironic side effect of this weapons buildup, however—spending billions of dollars amassing weapons of mass destruction was extremely beneficial to the U.S. economy.

Meanwhile, children of the baby boom generation were forced to confront the fact that they might be annihilated by nuclear weapons at any moment. At school they practiced air raid drills, in which they were instructed to hide under their desks and put their hands over their heads—duck and cover—a futile gesture supposedly ensuring survival in the event of a nuclear attack. And they were taught to despise and fear communists in newspapers, magazines, movies, and television shows.

With most Americans expecting a destructive war with the Soviet Union, fear of communist infiltration into the highest reaches of the American government created a climate of near panic. By the mid-1950s, people who were branded communist could lose their jobs, their homes, and even be put into prison. This label was applied to many who did not fit into white middle-class society, including blacks fighting for equal rights, Jewish intellectuals, union organizers, college professors, artists, musicians, poets, and activists of all kinds.

While some Americans approved of the anticommunist witch hunts, many baby boomers heard cynicism in their parents' complaints about the heavy-handed tactics of the government, which some accused of manipulating the communist threat to harass those deemed undesirable. By the late fifties public opinion had turned against the shrill anti-communist rhetoric of senators and congressmen, some of whom were exposed as corrupt hypocrites during televised congressional hearings. This harsh brand of take-no-prisoners politics served as a political awakening for record numbers of baby boomers who were well into their teens.

Racial Discord

While cold war militarism was boosting the postwar economy to unprecedented levels, the United States was experiencing a sharp economic divide between prosperous middle-class whites and poor black African Americans. Black people in the United States had been living under a discriminatory legal policy known as "separate but equal" since the late nineteenth century, a policy that fostered very little equality.

Throughout the fifties and early sixties schools that black children attended were often funded at 10 percent of the levels of white schools. Laws in southern states mandated that

Martin Luther King Jr., shown here addressing a group of protesters in Atlanta, was an instrumental leader of the civil rights movement.

African Americans use different streetcars, restrooms, schools, parks, movie theaters, restaurants, water fountains, and other facilities from those used by white people. These so-called Jim Crow laws, named after a nineteenth-century racist song, also prevented black people from voting.

When civil rights marchers attempted to integrate southern cities and obtain fair voting practices they were jailed, beaten, and murdered. Images of black protesters being violently sprayed by fire hoses and attacked by police dogs were printed in magazines and broadcast on television sets across the country. Thousands of white baby boomers saw these pictures and lent their support to the protesters. Some even traveled to the South to spend their summer vacations marching arm-in-arm with black civil rights workers.

Baby boomers who experienced the civil rights movement firsthand often absorbed information and attitudes about the struggle for racial equality and returned to colleges across the country ready to spread the message. On nearly every large college campus white students formed organizations to support black civil rights and end discrimination in housing and the workplace.

College and Vietnam

It was a well-educated, well-to-do group of white students who lent their support to the civil rights movement. And the baby boomers were the first generation to graduate from high school in such large numbers. In 1900, for example, only 6.4 percent of young Americans completed high school. At the beginning of World War II, most young people were working full-time by the age of eighteen. Only 20 percent of American teens graduated from high school in that era, while little more than 16 percent went on to college. In the 1960s, however, over 90 percent of baby boomers were high school graduates and about 50 percent went to college. In 1900 there were about 238,000 college students; in 1970 there were 7 million, and by 1980 there were 10 million.

Then, just as the first baby boomers began to turn eighteen in 1964, U.S. involvement in Vietnam escalated, which required the military to draft millions of young people. Utilizing tactics learned in the black civil rights struggle, resistance to the war was almost immediate on campuses across the country. As the war continued, hundreds of thousands of boomers created pandemonium in the streets protesting American involvement in Vietnam. This was arguably the first time in history that millions of people seriously questioned their own government's choices in fighting a war.

The numbers help explain the phenomenon. In 1964, with a U.S. population of about 192 million, seventeen-year-olds composed the largest age group in the country, and 24 million people were between the ages of fifteen and twenty-four. By 1970 that number had grown to 35 million. By 1966, almost 50 percent of the people in America were under the age of twenty-six. The term "generation gap" was coined to describe the often violent disagreements between these young people and their parents and other authority figures about the government that represented them in a country where the voting age was twenty-one.

The Psychedelic Sixties

The war was only one divisive issue that widened the generation gap. The sixties were a time of riots in inner-city neighborhoods and assassinations of political leaders such as President John F. Kennedy; his brother, presidential candidate Robert Kennedy; and civil rights leader Martin Luther King Jr.

Adding to this social volatility was the widespread availability of drugs: During the 1960s, for the first time significant numbers of Americans began to experiment with psychedelics such as peyote, marijuana, mescaline, and LSD. In fact, by the end of the sixties, nearly 6 million baby boomers from junior high school students to rock stars had taken LSD. And up to 20 million—more than one in four baby boomers—had smoked pot.

The psychedelic revolution had its roots in San Francisco, where best-selling author Ken Kesey staged "acid tests" in which LSD was given to hundreds of people at huge all-night dance parties. People decorated their bodies with Day-glo paint, watched protoplasmic light shows, and danced all night to the psychedelic rock of the Grateful Dead and other bands. The media publicity surrounding Kesey's acid tests spread LSD use far beyond San Francisco, and a psychedelic revolution quickly overtook America. Suburban teens grew long hair, donned love beads and tie-dyed T-shirts, took drugs, and began to seriously question their parents' materialistic values.

Not surprisingly during this era, rock music in all its forms continued to dominate the lives of the baby boomers. Bob Dylan, the Beatles, Jimi Hendrix, Cream, Janis Joplin, the Jefferson Airplane, and thousands of other acts filled the air with songs of love, peace, and revolution.

The psychedelic hippie dream culminated in a field in Bethel, New York, between August 15 and 17, 1969, at the Woodstock Music and Art Festival. Fifty thousand attendees were expected, but when nearly half a million baby boomers showed up to listen to the top rock acts of the sixties, the festival turned into a giant "love-in." Despite little food, few bathrooms, and severe rainstorms, there were few fights and no murders. There was, however, an overwhelming sense of power as the baby boomers of the so-called Woodstock Nation envisioned a future marked by cooperation and social harmony.

Permanent Changes

Although counterculture antics and the antiwar movement dominated headlines in the sixties, not all baby boomers were hippies and revolutionaries. Some supported the war in Vietnam and went to fight in the jungles of Southeast Asia. Most simply lived their lives, going to school, working at jobs, and fulfilling their responsibilities. But the dream of Woodstock profoundly affected a majority of the generation. In a 1980 survey, 70 percent of baby boomers interviewed said they wished they had gone to Woodstock. And the idealism of the festival affected people in other ways. According to Anthony M. Casale and Philip Lerman in *Where Have All the Flowers Gone? The Fall and Rise of the Woodstock Generation:*

> [The] spirit of Woodstock did not die. It would begin to resurface in subtle ways, blending with more traditional val-

ues . . . to form a more tolerant and energetic nation. It's as if you took the spirit of Woodstock, eliminated most of the naiveté, and sprinkled in some political savvy. Some may call it simply getting older and wiser.

People [in later decades] began subtly . . . to reject authority. Protests surfaced, but mainly in a different form. People translated their need for independence into new lifestyles, job styles, new types of entrepreneurism. Minorities, women, gays, the elderly, and others expected to be heard. That was true whether you were a straight or a freak, a shorthair or a longhair. The young people of the 1960s had pretty well separated the country into Us and Them, but as they grew older they learned that Us and Them had more in common than they thought.[5]

Women's Liberation

The counterculture movement began to splinter in the early seventies. Millions of female baby boomers, however, came together to demand equal rights for women. They had learned the protest tactics of the sixties and turned them on both their former allies and the Establishment. And in a stunning series of victories, women forced society to confront attitudes that had repressed females for centuries.

Between 1972 and 1975, thirty-three states ratified the Equal Rights Amendment to the Constitution—first proposed in 1923—that simply stated: "Equality of rights under the law shall not be denied or abridged by the United States or any state on account of sex." Although the amendment failed to win ratification by the necessary majority, in the face of strong opposition organized to defeat it, it was an exhilarating time for supporters of women's rights.

In January 1973 the Supreme Court legalized abortion, which had been illegal in all states except California and New York. For the rest of the era, boomer women led the fight for reproductive rights, equal pay for equal work, and the right of women to work at jobs traditionally held by men.

The media quickly picked up on women's liberation and moved it into the mainstream of American culture. Newspapers and news magazines did cover stories on the gender inequality in American society. Suddenly words such as *sexism* and *chauvinism* were part of daily language. And when the women's magazine *Ms.* was launched in 1972, its 300,000 copies sold out in only eight days while garnering an unheard-of 26,000 subscription orders and 20,000 letters to the editor.

Television broadcasts followed the trend. TV programs such as *The Mary Tyler Moore Show* and *Mary Hartman, Mary Hartman* featured strong-willed, free-thinking women who became role models for young girls.

During the 1970s, many baby boomers started families of

Betty Friedan, cofounder of the National Organization for Women, was a leader in the campaign to ratify the Equal Rights Amendment.

their own, and some began to shift their focus to healthy living and leaving the world a better place for their children. Even before the Vietnam War ended in 1975, the environmental movement had grown at a rapid pace as boomers began to worry about air and water pollution. At the same time, eating a healthier diet became important and thousands of boomers began to shop at food co-ops and health food stores where organic produce and minimally processed products were sold.

The seventies also saw major disruptions in the American economy. Boomers who had been raised in the best economy in history were shocked by midseventies gasoline shortages and uncontrolled inflation, which was led by a doubling of oil prices. By the end of the decade, interest rates were over 21 percent, putting the dream of homeownership out of reach for many boomers just starting families.

The faltering economy also caused unemployment rates to skyrocket just as millions of baby boomers were graduating from college and entering the job market. For those suffering through the worst recession since the 1930s, simply working, feeding a growing family, and paying mounting bills made many put their sixties ideals behind them.

Gas shortages, unemployment, rising housing costs, and other problems showed baby boomers that their idealistic expectations could quickly fall to pieces against the concrete reality of adult life.

A Move to the Right

By the 1980s, the liberal ideals of the baby boom generation had become the target of a growing conservative movement. The 1980 election of right-wing Republican Ronald Reagan proved that the World War II generation remained firmly in control of the government and economy. But three-quarters of the baby boomers who voted in the election supported the conservative Reagan.

The Reagan administration quickly rolled back environmental protection regulations, revitalized the war on drugs, cut budgets to welfare and housing agencies, slashed taxes to stimulate the economy, and started the biggest defense buildup in history.

Though many baby boomers disagreed with his politics, Reagan was perceived as exuding a sunny optimism that boosted America's confidence in itself after a decade of gas lines, hyperinflation, layoffs, and shattered dreams.

Growing older and more conservative in the 1980s, the baby boomers continued to change the fabric of American life. Their quest for material wealth coincided with a booming eighties economy. The term "yuppie" was invented to label the young urban professionals who were boosting sales of luxury cars, diamonds, furs, and expensive wine.

In 1984 a *Newsweek* cover story touted the arrival of the year of the yuppie. The sixties ideals of sharing and caring were replaced, as Casale and Lerman write, by "achieving, striving, and buying. Suddenly everything was work: working hard and working out and working within the system; working mothers and working relationships; working the phone and working the room and working the nightshift."[6]

This increase in productivity was fueled by a high-tech computer revolution that also had its roots in the baby boom

Though many baby boomers disagreed with Ronald Reagan's policies, three-quarters of them voted for him in the 1980 presidential election.

generation: Whiz kids such as Microsoft founder Bill Gates, Apple founder Steve Jobs, and others built multibillion-dollar empires from scratch.

While many Americans prospered financially in the 1980s, there were three major recessions between 1982 and 1992. In addition, inflation completely changed baby boomers' ability to afford a middle-class lifestyle. Between 1972 and 1987 the average price for a new home increased from about $29,000 to almost $83,000—an increase of 294 percent. A monthly mortgage payment leaped from $152 to $581. The cost of a new Chevrolet climbed from $3,700 to $11,800. As baby boomers moved through their thirties and forties, some realized that they could not achieve the material well-being that most of their parents had taken for granted.

Growing Older

In the 1990s, the first baby boomers turned fifty and began to think about retirement. Fueled by a high-tech boom and an influx of billions of dollars from retirement accounts, the stock market soared and many baby boomers were finally able to find financial security.

By 2000, however, Americans were beginning to come to terms with the fact that the largest and most influential generation in history was toddling into old age. As the high-tech stock bust dragged the stock market down—along with trillions of dollars in boomer retirement savings—Americans' Social Security system began to look like it would fail.

When Social Security was first implemented in the 1930s, the average American died before reaching his or her sixty-fifth birthday. In those days people collected monthly Social Security payments for at most a few years after they retired. Today, people are living longer than ever, and baby boomers who begin retiring in 2010 can expect to collect Social Security for an average of ten years or more. In the twenty years that will follow more people will be receiving benefits than there will be workers contributing to the system. By the year 2034, the system is projected to fall into bankruptcy just as long-living baby boomers hit their eighties and nineties.

Baby boomers will also cause a severe strain on the health

care system in the United States as they grow old and sick. Political battles will be waged between the boomers and younger people whose taxes will have to be drastically raised to support them.

In the End

Today, baby boomers remain the largest demographic group in American history and continue to affect society for better or for worse. As Paul C. Light writes in *Baby Boomers:*

> To the extent seventy-five million people think alike, they define the contemporary culture. To the extent they buy alike, they shape the economy. To the extent they are both preceded and followed by much smaller generations, they stand out in sharp contrast to those around them.[7]

Light's words, however, reveal the danger of trying to assign 75 million people to neat stereotypical categories. Baby boomers are men, women, black, white, Hispanic, Asian, and Native American. They are Christians, Jews, Buddhists, Muslims, and members of dozens of other religions. Some are socially conservative, many are politically centrist, and a few have retained the rebellious attitudes of the sixties. Baby boomers are rich, poor, and middle class.

In spite of their differences, the baby boom generation grew up in a time of nationally shared experiences. There were only three major television stations until the 1970s, no cable TV, and no personal computers. For more than twenty years, almost all Americans watched the same TV shows and experienced major news events as a giant community. Almost everyone remembers where they were on November 22, 1963, when President John F. Kennedy was assassinated in Dallas. Similarly, they remember Woodstock and other cultural watersheds.

Boomers will age and their influence will wane; someday they will be gone, like all those who came before them. While they have been derided as a spoiled generation who continue to dominate American culture long after middle age, boomers have forever changed the world. The fight for equal rights among all races, women, and gays are part of the baby boom legacy. The environmental movement and the digital revolution also have their roots in the baby boom generation.

Through a series of historical coincidences, the baby boomers lived through an era of unprecedented growth and technological advancement. And they were able to shape the world through sheer numbers. Baby boomers are parents, grandparents, and even great-grandparents. They have much to teach and much to learn. And in that, they are little different from all who were born before or since.

Notes

1. William Sterling and Stephen Waite, *Boomernomics*. New York: Library of Contemporary Thought, 1998, p. 2.

2. Kenneth Keniston, *Young Radicals: Notes on Committed Youth*. New York: Harcourt, Brace & World, 1968, p. 235.

3. Quoted in David Halberstam, *The Fifties*. New York: Villard, 1993, p. 471.

4. Bruce Pollock, *Hipper than Our Kids*. New York: Schirmer, 1993, pp. 2–3.

5. Anthony M. Casale and Philip Lerman, *Where Have All the Flowers Gone? The Fall and Rise of the Woodstock Generation*. Kansas City, MO: Andrews and McMeel, 1989, p. 4.

6. Casale and Lerman, *Where Have All the Flowers Gone?* p. 142.

7. Paul C. Light, *Baby Boomers*. New York: W.W. Norton, 1988, p. 9.

Chapter 1

The Beginning of the Boom

Turning | Points
IN WORLD HISTORY

A Booming Baby Explosion

Landon Y. Jones

After World War II, the birth rate in America surged to record numbers, fueling an economic miracle that lasted until the 1970s. Growing families created expanding markets for new housing, automobiles, toys, televisions, and even new ways of eating such as TV dinners and fast food restaurants. Before the war most Americans lived in small apartments in big cities. By 1960, more than 60 million people, or one-third of the population, moved to suburbs that had not even existed before the fifties. As Landon Y. Jones, senior editor at *People* magazine writes, this drastic increase in population completely changed the economic and social makeup of America in a few short years.

In the early 1950s, the huge Census Clock in Washington was clicking like a runaway taxi meter. Every seven seconds the Birth Light blinked off a new baby. Boys were arriving with familiar names like Robert, John, James, Michael, William, Richard, Joseph, Thomas, Steven, and David, making a Top Ten of favorite names that was proudly all-American. Girls were named Linda, Mary, Barbara, Patricia, Susan, Kathleen, Carol, Nancy, Margaret, and Diane. And perhaps thanks to [actress] Debbie Reynolds, "Deborah" would have a run all of her own later in the decade.

Like the steel industry, mothering was running at close to 100 percent capacity, and it was harder and harder to keep up. In January of 1952, General Electric decided to celebrate its seventy-fifth anniversary by awarding five shares of common stock to any employee who had a baby on October 15. Some public-relations whiz tried to predict the eventual number of winners by dividing the total of 226,000 G.E. employees by the U.S. crude birthrate. Unfortunately, he forgot that G.E. workers as a population were considerably more fertile than the United States as a whole, since they contained no one under 17 nor over 65. In the end, the company's guess that thirteen G.E. babies would be born amounted to underestimation on a grand scale. The workers, true to the thriving surplus economy of the era, came through with no less than 189 new G.E. babies that day.

But General Electric was not about to complain. It was investing $650 million in new plants and assembly lines over seven postwar years to prepare for the boom in babies. As early as 1948, *Time* noted that the U.S. population had just increased by "2,800,000 more consumers" *(not* babies) the year before. Economists happily predicted that the new babies would set off a demand explosion for commodities such as homes, foodstuffs, clothing, furniture, appliances, and schools, to name only a few examples. *Fortune* pronounced the baby boom "exhilarating" and with an almost-audible sigh of relief concluded that the low birthrates of the 1930s were a "freakish interlude, rather than a trend." "We need not stew too much about a post-[World War II] depression," the magazine wrote. "A civilian market growing by the size of Iowa every year ought to be able to absorb whatever production the military will eventually turn loose."

As the economic and baby booms surged on together, the cheerleading became almost feverish. Public-service signs went up in New York City subways reading, "Your future is great in a growing America. Every day 11,000 babies are born in America. This means new business, new jobs, new opportunities." After-dinner speakers began to talk about "Prosperity by Population" and lofted tantalizing guesses of up to five million new babies a year by 1975. Financial magazines editorialized about the joys of "this remarkable boom." "Gone, for the first time in history," announced *Time* in 1955, "is the worry over whether a society can produce enough goods to take care of its people. The lingering worry is whether it will have enough people to consume the goods."

The most euphoric article of all, perhaps, was a story *Life* printed in 1958, at the height of the boom. Three dozen children were crowded onto the cover along with the banner head-line: KIDS: BUILT-IN RECESSION CURE—HOW 4,000,000 A YEAR MAKE MILLIONS IN BUSINESS. Inside, the article began with an-other headline—ROCKETING BIRTHS: BUSINESS BONANZA—and continued chockablock with statistics and photographs about new citizens who were "a brand-new market for food, clothing, and shelter." In its first year, *Life* calculated, a baby is not just a child but already a prodigious consumer, "a po-tential market for $800 worth of products." Even before re-turning from the hospital, an infant had "already rung up $450 in medical expenses." Four-year-olds are not just sugar and spice or puppy-dog tails but rather represent "a backlog of business orders that will take two decades to fulfill." A rhapsodic *Life* then clinched its case by visiting Joe Powers, a thirty-five-year-old salesman from Port Washington, New York. He and his wife, Carol, had produced ten children and were buying 77 quarts of milk and 28 loaves of bread a week, just for starters. Faced with examples like that of meritorious devotion to the Procreation Ethic, little wonder that some American mothers felt as if it were their *duty* to have chil-dren. Either they were pregnant or, if not, wondered whether they should be.

The baby-boom kids had kicked off in America a bucca-neering orgy of buying and selling that carried all things be-fore it. The only thing like it earlier was the Gilded Age of the post-Civil War 1870s, which the historian Vernon Louis Parrington so aptly dubbed "the Great Barbecue." Here was a feast spread out for an entire nation, and everyone scram-bling for it. More food was spoiled than eaten, perhaps, and the revelry was a bit unseemly, but no one minded. Every-where people were getting rich in a demographic debauch.

The spending boom started, literally, at the bottom. Dia-pers went from a $32-million industry in 1947 to $50 mil-lion in 1957. The diaper services (disposables had not yet ar-rived) also prospered. Mothers and fathers were paying $5 million annually (twice the preboom business) to have baby's shoes bronze-plated at L.E. Mason, Inc., in Boston. The under-5 appetite, which had grown from 13 million mouths to 20 million by 1960, more than one out of every ten Americans, was consuming baby food at a rate of 1.5 billion cans a year in 1953 (up from 270 million cans in 1940).

As the kids grew up, so did the markets. Throughout the 1950s, the 5–13 age group grew by an additional one million baby boomers every year. The toy industry set sales records annually after 1940, growing from an $84-million-a-year stripling to a $1.25-billion giant. Sales of bicycles doubled to two million a year; cowboy outfits became a $75-million subindustry; space-science toys claimed another $60 million. Children's clothes became a boom market, and packaging researchers suddenly discovered the troika of "family" sizes—Giant, Economy, and Supereconomy. At its peak, the juvenile market was ringing up a staggering $33 billion annually.

Suburban "Babyvilles"

The rain of spending did not fall evenly on society. Rather, it was both a cause and an effect of what amounted to the opening of a new American frontier: the suburbs. Historians had already suggested that America's expansiveness during the nineteenth century was built on the common goal of settling the West. Now there was a new impetus behind the conquering of the suburban frontier: babies. The suburbs were conceived for the baby boom—and vice versa. Here in green garlands around the cities, Americans were creating new child-oriented societies, "babyvilles" teeming with new appetites, new institutions, and new values. Families who were asked why they moved to the suburbs first mentioned better housing and leisure, as if they were conforming to the old goal of a country place that began with the French aristocracy. But then, invariably, they added that they thought suburbia was "a better place to bring up the kids." The common acceptance of this goal united the suburbs. "Instead of the wagon train, where people leaned on one another as they moved across the continent," historian Daniel Boorstin remarked, "Americans in suburbs leaned on one another as they moved rapidly about the country and up the ladder of consumption." Author William H. Whyte found the same communal spirit in his examination of the mythical suburb of Park Forest. Families shared baby-sitters, cribs, lawn mowers, tea services, and baseball equipment. "We laughed at first at how the Marxist society had finally arrived," one suburban executive told Whyte. "But I think the real analogy is to the pioneers."

As an internal migration, the settling of the suburbs was phenomenal. In the twenty years from 1950 to 1970, the population of the suburbs doubled from 36 million to 72 million. No less than 83 percent of the total population

---

Women Married Younger

The baby boom began in the late 1940s when women married earlier and started families at a younger age, as freelance journalist Brett Harvey describes in the following excerpt.

In the years following World War II, Americans married in record numbers. In 1940, 31 percent of the population was single; by 1950, that number had dropped to 23 percent, and by 1960, to 21 percent. They also married younger than ever: During the 1950s, the median marriage age dropped from 24.3 to 22.6 for men, and from 21.5 to 20.4 for women. (By contrast, the median marriage ages for men and women in 1990 were, respectively, 26.1 and 23.9.) But even these statistics don't quite do justice to the strength of the trend. By 1959, a staggering 47 percent of all brides were married before the age of nineteen. Another 1959 study revealed that two out of three women who entered college dropped out— usually to get married.

Once married, Americans began their families almost immediately. Women who came of age in the fifties had an average of 3.2 children, and most couples had completed their families by their late twenties. And contrary to popular belief, educated women were in the forefront of the trend. The notion that, in the words of a 1946 *Newsweek* article, "For the American girl books and babies don't mix," persisted in spite of clear evidence that the steepest increase in the birthrate occurred among highly educated women.

Brett Harvey, *The Fifties: A Women's Oral History.* New York: HarperCollins, 1993.

growth in the United States during the 1950s was in the sub-urbs, which were growing fifteen times faster than any other segment of the country. As people packed and moved, the national mobility rate leaped by 50 percent. The only other comparable influx was the wave of European immigrants to the United States around the turn of the century. But, as *Fortune* pointed out, more people moved to the suburbs every year than had ever arrived on Ellis Island.

By now, bulldozers were churning up dust storms as they cleared the land for housing developments. More than a million acres of farmland were plowed under every year during the 1950s. Millions of apartment-dwelling parents with two children were suddenly realizing that two children could be doubled up in a spare bedroom, but a third child cried loudly for something more. The proportion of new houses with three or more bedrooms, in fact, rose from one-third in 1947 to three-quarters by 1954. The necessary [room for people] could only be found in the suburbs. There was a housing shortage, but young couples armed with VA and FHA loans built their dream homes with easy credit and free spending habits that were unthinkable to the baby-boom grandparents, who shook their heads with the Depression still fresh in their memories. Of the 13 million homes built in the decade before 1958, 11 million of them—or 85 percent—were built in the suburbs. Home ownership rose 50 percent between 1940 and 1950, and another 50 per-cent by 1960. By then, one-fourth of *all* housing in the United States had been built in the fifties. For the first time, more Americans owned homes than rented them.

We were becoming a land of gigantic nurseries. The biggest were built by Abraham Levitt, the son of poor Russian-Jewish immigrants, who had originally built houses for the Navy during the war. The first of three East Coast Levittowns went up on the potato fields of Long Island. Ex-actly $7990—or $60 a month and no money down—bought you a Monopoly-board bungalow with four rooms, attic, washing machine, outdoor barbecue, and a television set built into the wall. The 17,447 units eventually became home to 82,000 people, many of whom were pregnant or wanted to be. In a typical story on the suburban explosion, one magazine breathlessly described a volleyball game of nine couples in which no less than five of the women were expecting.

Washing Machines and Cars

Marketers were quick to spot what amounted to capitalism's Klondike Lode. "Anybody who wants to sell anything to Americans should take a long look at the New Suburbia," marveled *Fortune* in 1953. "It is big and lush and uniform— a combination made to order for the comprehending marketer." It went far beyond toys and diapers. In suburbia's servantless society, laborsaving devices were necessary adjuncts to having children. The number of washing machines sold in America went from 1.7 million in 1950 to 2.6 million in 1960. Sales of electric clothes dryers doubled during one two-year stretch. With a then-astonishing average family income of $6500 (compared to $3800 for everyone else), the suburbanites were creating an American way of spending organized around children and the needs they created. Retailers eagerly followed them to the suburbs, opening branch stores by the dozen and clearing the way for the later age of shopping malls.

The settlers of suburbia also brought with them beasts of burden. They had Fords in their future—and Chevys and De Sotos and Hudsons and Studebakers. The car, especially the second car, was the one indispensable suburban accessory. Car registrations soared along with the birthrate: from 26 million in 1945 to 40 million in 1950 to 60 million by the end of the decade. The number of two-car families rose 750,000 a year and doubled from 1951 to 1958. Station wagons, the housewife's version of the [army's] Willys Jeep, began crisscrossing the suburbs like water bugs, dropping off husbands, picking up children, stopping by the supermarket. "A suburban mother's role is to deliver children obstetrically once," said Peter De Vries, "and by car forever after." *Time* joked that "if the theory of evolution is still working, it may well one day transform the suburban housewife's right foot into a flared paddle, grooved for easy traction on the gas pedal and brake."

Even in those days, the automobile had seized its central place in the emotional life of the baby boom. It was the first entire generation to be driven before it walked. It was the first generation to grow up in cars, even to seek its entertainment in cars. Back in 1933 a chemicals manufacturer named Richard Hollinshead had turned a parking lot in Camden, New Jersey, into the World's First Automobile Movie Theatre. Fifteen years later, there were only 480 drive-ins in the country. But between 1948 and 1958 the number zoomed to 4000, equipped with everything from playgrounds for the kids to Laundromats for Mom. For millions of baby-boom parents, a night at the drive-in neatly solved the suburban dilemma of what to do if you couldn't get a baby-sitter. Much later, the adolescent baby boomers would find their own use for the passion pits. Here is Lisa Alther in *Kinflicks:*

> Mixed with the dialogue were the various sighs and gasps and sucking sounds from the front seats and blasts from car horns throughout the parking area as, in keeping with Hullsport High tradition, couples signalled that they'd gone all the way.

Nowhere was the postwar baby-suburb-car symbiosis more symbolically apparent than during the gasoline shortage of July 1979 in the Philadelphia suburb of Levittown, Pennsylvania. There some 75,000 people live on 7000 acres of suburb. But, for a city of such density, it is served by little mass transportation. Threatened by the loss of their cars, angry young Levittowners staged the nation's first gas riot, burning cars, stoning ambulances, and battling police. Ironically, many of the 195 who were arrested belonged to the same families who had originally settled there during the baby-boom years and who, in 1960, won the Little League World Series for Levittown.

Meanwhile, the suburbs continued to grow and prosper and create a whole new sequence of bench marks for American Studies teachers. In 1956, white-collar [office] workers outnumbered blue-collar [factory] workers for the first time. In 1970, the suburbs became the largest single sector of the nation's population, exceeding both central cities and the farms. By 1972, the suburbs were even offering more jobs than the central cities. Everyone was enthusiastically buying "on time" (as it was called then), and the number of Americans who thought installment financing was a good thing increased from 50 percent to 60 percent in ten years.

Sociologists began to pursue the suburbanites like doctors after a new virus. The baby-boom parents were poked and prodded and examined with the kind of fascination hitherto reserved for South Sea Islanders. They were, to be sure, pioneering a life-style (the dread word first came into currency then) that would be predominant in America. Often living in small houses filled with children, they moved outside to their patios and barbecue pits and created a new, rigorously informal style. Lawn and porch furniture sales went from $53 million in 1950 to $145 million in 1960. Hot dog production likewise zoomed from 750 million pounds to more than 2 billion pounds in the decade. Everyone first-named everyone and no one criticized the neighbor's kids (at least in front of a neighbor). . . .

Some of these studies no doubt revealed more of the anxieties of the examiners than the examined. (Did ordinary citizens really have "identity crises"?) But, if there was a common message, it was of the *sameness* of suburbia. It was as if the same forces that produced prosperity and fertility also produced [bland conformity]. Parents had rediscovered the old verities—home, hearth, children, church. But they had also made a faith out of brand names, modular housing, and gray flannel suits. Everywhere were the same drugstores, the same franchises, the same music on the radio. The children, too, were being shaped by a world of repeatable experience. But they were not being molded by their parents or their teachers. Instead, there was another dominant presence in the early lives of the baby boomers. It was one that would forge their unity as a generation. It would mobilize them as a consumer force. It was television. In 1938, E.B. White prophesied that "television is going to be the test of the modern world and . . . in this new opportunity to see beyond the range of our vision we shall discover either a new and unbearable disturbance of the general peace or a saving radiance in the sky. We shall stand or fall by television—of that I am quite sure." In the year White wrote that, barely 2 percent of American families owned the small, flickering Philcos and DuMonts dwarfed in their elephantine cabinets. But in less than a decade, the age of television swept over us. From fewer than 6000 sets manufactured at the baby boom's outset in 1946, production leaped, almost impossibly, to 7 million a year by 1953. Eighty-six percent of American homes had television sets at the end of the decade and, by 1967, 98 percent of all homes had sets, effectively saturating the market. The exponential growth curve of television was steeper than that of any other technological innovation of the century—including the telephone, radio, and automobile.

It was also the most important new child-care development of the century, one that would redefine the environment in which Americans grew up. Some of the oldest baby-boomers remember when the first sets were lugged into their homes. But, for most, television was not an intruder in the home but . . . "the third parent," practically a family member itself. These children treated the glowing box not with the awe due a mysterious and wonderful invention but with the unquestioned familiarity of an old armchair or the kitchen sink.

The First TV Generation

Paul C. Light

Baby boomers were the first generation in history to be raised in front of the television, and ever since the early fifties, politicians, social scientists, and others have been questioning the influence of TV viewing on children. As professor of political science Paul C. Light explains, television had both good and bad effects on baby boomers.

"Television itself is a baby boomer, it's a baby-boom instrument," [former] NBC chief Brandon Tartikoff said. "The baby-boom generation has never known a living environment in which there wasn't a television." By the time the average baby boomer reached age 16, he or she had watched from 12,000 to 15,000 hours of TV, or the equivalent of 24 hours a day for 15 to 20 solid months. . . .

"The impact of television on this generation so far exceeds the impact of radio, motion pictures, and vaudeville on previous generations because of the universality of TV," says Mike Dann, former CBS programming head. "It has had a profound impact on the speech patterns, the dress, and to some extent the intellectual process of any number of people growing up even in the earliest days of television."

Looking back to the 1950s and 1960s, television affected the baby boomers in three distinctive ways. First, from the very beginning, it separated them from traditional social connections, and taught them intimate lessons about being an adult without any intervention from parents or teachers. Second, it presented a world of remarkable similarity from channel to channel, a "vast wasteland" as Federal Communications Commission (FCC) chairman Newton Minnow . . . called it [in 1961]. Third, and perhaps most important, if TV

From *Baby Boomers*, by Paul C. Light. Copyright © 1988 by Paul Charles Light. Used by permission of W.W. Norton & Company, Inc.

violence did not create a pathological generation, it may have created a sense of fear about the world.

Television is both a crowded medium, with multiple cuts of information packed between strict time boundaries, and an intimate medium, to be watched alone even in a crowded room. Sociologist Robert Bellah and his colleagues believe that the combination fosters social separation through the sheer succession of sensations: "But television operates not only with a complete disconnectedness between successive programs. Even within a single hour or half-hour program, there is extraordinary discontinuity. Commercials regularly break whatever mood has built up with their own, often very different emotional message. Even aside from commercials, television style is singularly abrupt and jumpy, with many quick cuts to other scenes and other characters. Dialogue is reduced to clipped sentences. No one talks long enough to express anything complex. Depth of feeling, if it exists at all, has to be expressed in a word or a glance."

NBC officially opens its television studio at Rockefeller Center in New York City on April 22, 1948.

To the extent television gave the young baby boomers this mix of fixed time boundaries and social separation simultaneously, it reinforced the generation's separation from potential societal networks. There can be little doubt that television reduced the baby boom's contact with its peers and parents, and that the generation made its first contacts with the real world through the medium. Data from the early days of television support these ideas. "Even at the age of three," scholars Wilbur Schramm, Jack Lyle, and Edwin Parker argued in 1961, "when the average viewing time is in the neighborhood of 45 minutes a day, the child spends more time on television than even on hearing stories." It also produced a drop in the amount of time spent playing either alone or with other children, and reduced the time spent in conversation and family interaction, another privation of experience.

More important, it crowded out other sources of information and pleasure. Nine out of ten baby boomers were well acquainted with TV long before they read their first newspaper. Two-thirds were active TV viewers before they saw their first movie. Moreover, television was the baby boom's window on world events. For example, it eventually became the major source for their knowledge about the war in Vietnam, far more so than for their parents or teachers, and it may have eclipsed the family as a source of political information. One political scientist even maintains that television became a new social parent in the 1960s. Recall the question of why parents did not pass on their party loyalty to their children. Perhaps one answer is that TV got in the way.

A Magic Doorway

Why were the baby boomers captured? Because, as Schramm and his colleagues concluded, television was "first, and always predominantly, a magic doorway into a world of fantasy, glamour, and excitement. It is an invitation to relax, to disregard one's real-life problems, to surrender oneself to the charming and handsome people, the absorbing events, that flicker on the picture tube." In that regard, television was to the baby boomers what comics had been to their parents. Yet, unlike comics, television introduced the baby boomers to a very adult world. As Schramm and his coauthors continued, "a very large proportion of children's television viewing is of adult programs. The effect of this is that the old timetable for gradually exposing a child to adult ideas is gone forever. There is no use looking nostalgically back toward it—it is gone."

Long before Vietnam [in the sixties] and double-digit inflation [in the 1970s], the question of whether the baby boom's reality would ever be able to match the fantasy world of television was asked by child psychiatrist Eugene Glynn. "These children are in a peculiar position," Glynn wrote in the mid-1950s, "experience is exhausted in advance. There is little they have not seen or done or lived through, and yet this is secondhand experience. When the experience itself comes, it is watered down, for it has already been half lived but never truly felt." In one sense, the baby boom was long composed of little adults, asked to think about the big questions long before they had the capacity to find the answers.

Television also offered baby boomers very few choices for viewing across the channels. Lower and upper classes, boys and girls, blacks and whites all shared the same programs. As Minnow told an assembly of broadcasters in May 1961, "I invite you to sit down in front of your television set when your station goes on the air and stay there without a book, magazine, newspaper, profit-and-loss sheet or rating book to distract you—and keep your eyes glued to that set until the station signs off. I can assure that you will observe a vast wasteland." According to Minnow, television was little more than "a procession of game shows, violence, audience-participation shows, formula comedies about totally unbelievable families, blood and thunder, mayhem, violence, sadism, murder, Western bad men, Western good men, private eyes, gangsters, more violence, screaming, cajoling and offending. And most of all boredom."

Fewer Program Types

The program schedules proved his point. Examining all 2,000 prime-time programs from 1953 to 1974, journalism professors Joseph Dominick and Millard Pearce concluded that programming became more similar over time. Action adventures were increasingly popular, growing from just 10 percent of all programs in 1953 to just over half by 1960. Movies were second, capturing almost 25 percent of all prime time by 1974, while situation comedies held steady at 20 percent throughout the period.

What this meant was that all baby boomers saw the same programs regardless of the channel they were watching. During the 1950s and 1960s, according to Dominick and Pearce, "more and more program time was being devoted to fewer and fewer program types. In 1954, for example, three categories—action/adventure, movies, and general drama—accounted for 81 percent of prime time." By 1964, action adventures had crowded out the general drama, leaving the baby boomers with even fewer choices. As network profits went up, diversity of programming went down. The authors noted, "the more money the industry made, the more the prime-time schedules on the networks began to resemble one another." Whatever the station, the baby boomers were likely to see the same shows—if not the "Munsters" then "Addams Family," if not "Bonanza" then "Gunsmoke."

Mixed into the baby boom's programming was a staggering amount of televised violence. While television showed a world of excitement and fantasy, it also showed a world of violence and risk. Take the following list from the week of October, 1961, as an example:

Twelve murders,

Sixteen major gunfights,

Twenty-one persons shot (apparently not fatally),

Twenty-one other violent incidents with guns (ranging from shooting at but missing persons, to shooting up a town),

Thirty-seven hand-to-hand fights (fifteen fist fights, fifteen incidents in which one person slugged another, an attempted murder with a pitchfork, two stranglings, a fight in the water, a case in which a woman was gagged and tied to a bed, and so forth),

One stabbing in the back with a butcher knife,

Four attempted suicides, three successful,

Four people falling or pushed over cliffs,

Two cars running over cliffs,

Two attempts made in automobiles to run over persons on the sidewalk,

A psychotic loose and raving in a flying airliner,

Two mob scenes, in one of which the mob hangs the wrong man,

A horse grinding a man under its hooves,

A great deal of miscellaneous violence, including a plane fight, a hired killer stalking his prey, two robberies, a pick-pocket working, a woman killed by falling from a train, a tidal wave, an earthquake, and a guillotining.

Darkened World of Anxiety

The question frequently raised is whether such scenes of violence had an impact on the baby boom. Some have argued, for example, that TV violence creates imitation and aggression in children. The evidence for that conclusion is sparse. According to Harvard scholars James Q. Wilson and Richard Hernstein, studies that try to measure very short-term effects (i.e., watching certain programs for a week or two) on behavior that is hard to observe (aggression) "are inevitably going to produce modest findings surrounded by many qualifications."

After two decades of research, the most that can be concluded is that violence on the air appears to be related to a short-term sense of anxiety and potential for aggression. That conclusion is some distance from a clear cause-and-effect relationship. "Were the facts known," Wilson and Hernstein argue, "it might be the case that merely being addicted to television, regardless of its contents, so poaches the brain or predisposes viewers to immediate gratification that they become unable to work for distant goals or engage in disciplined activity. It might then make engaging in crime (not necessarily violent crime) somewhat more likely, other things being equal."

Others have argued that television violence creates heightened fears about the outside world. "Compared to light viewers," Landon Jones wrote summarizing the research, "heavy television watchers live in a darkening world of anxiety. They greatly overestimate the proportion of people involved in violence, the danger of walking alone at night, and the number of criminals in society. . . . Heavy viewers are also more likely to mistrust the motives of other people and, when asked if it is all right to hit someone if you are mad at them, they answer 'almost always' in significantly higher proportions."

There was certainly enough TV violence in the 1950s and 1960s to feed baby-boom fears of a violent world. According to one study, violence was especially heavy during the late 1950s when TV cowboys ruled the range. Violent programs increased steadily from 20 percent of prime time in 1953 to 41 percent in 1959. The number fell in the early 1960s, but rose back up to near 40 percent by 1967.

Examining programming content from 1967 to 1969, com-

The Television Code of Good Practices

In the early days of television, civic and religious groups pressured the government to strictly limit what could be shown on TV. The broadcast industry adopted "The Television Code of Good Practices," printed below, in order to stave off federal intervention in programming. This self-imposed code prevented early television shows from portraying racial injustice, divorce, or even married couples sleeping in the same bed.

It is the responsibility of television to bear constantly in mind that the audience is primarily a home audience, and consequently that television's relationship to the viewers is that between guest and host. . . .

Television and all who participate in it are jointly accountable to the American public for respect for the special needs of children, for community responsibility, for the advancement of education and culture, for the acceptability of the program materials chosen, for decency and decorum in production, and for propriety in advertising. This responsibility cannot be discharged by any given group of programs, but can be discharged only through the highest standards of respect for the American home, applied to every moment of every program presented by television.

Nina C. Leibman, *Living Room Lectures: The Fifties Family in Film and Television.* Austin: University of Texas Press, 1995.

munications expert George Gerbner discovered three trends. First, the number of acts of violence per program went down. Second, the number of programs with at least some violence stayed about the same. Third, the violence became more sophisticated and less lethal. "Mannix" was still a tough guy, but he committed fewer acts of violence per program and fewer people were killed. Little Joe was still willing to fight on "Bonanza," but he kept his gun in its holster longer.

Further, the risks of violence never abated. To the extent that the baby boomers interpreted television as something near to real life, they must have concluded that their futures were indeed risky. According to Gerbner, of the 762 leading characters in 1967–69, 516 were involved in some kind of violence, whether as victims, violents, or both: "Thus, the 'average' character's chance of being involved in some violence [was about] twice as good as his chance of not being involved." Of those involved, "more were involved as victims than as violents. Five in ten committed some violence, but six in ten suffered. Chances of suffering violence rather than escaping it were 1.5 to one." Gerbner concluded that the "overriding message is that of the risk of victimization."

Victimization

The figures are particularly threatening for women. In a curious inversion, as the networks cut back on violent programming in the late 1960s, women became almost exclusively objects of violence, rather than aggressive participators. The new ground rules were simple. First, women could no longer be violent themselves. Gone were the days when a scheming wife could poison or shoot her husband on "Perry Mason." Second, women could no longer be criminals. Gone were the days when a man and woman could rob a bank on "Hawaii Five-O." Third, women could no longer appear to deserve a violent end. Gone were the days when a vicious woman could be murdered by her battered spouse on "Alfred Hitchcock."

Yet, if women were written out of the aggressive roles, they still remained as random victims. With the bad women off the air, only good women could be victims—mothers, innocent bystanders, co-eds. As Gerbner noted, "the shift to-ward female victimization is not so much an aspect of defeat as of fear and suffering."

Violence became something that could happen to anyone, and not only to women who seemed to deserve it or to those who had chosen a life of risk. Baby-boom women could not help but conclude that the chances of escaping violence were slim indeed, which may explain why they are so much more likely than men to favor more federal spending on crime today. In 1985, for example, the gap between the genders on this issue was 11 points (75 percent to 64 percent) among 20- to 29-year-olds, and 15 points (78 percent versus 63 percent) between 30- to 39-year-olds.

As a result of their childhood TV viewing, the baby boomers entered adulthood with a much clearer sense of the risks of life, whether from the fantasy of television violence or from the reality of events like Vietnam. If television was a magic doorway to fantasy, it was also a frightening doorway to violence and fear. It was a doorway that most baby boomers passed through, regardless of their age, gender, education, or class.

A New Kind of Music

Douglas T. Miller and Marion Nowak

Rock and roll music has become so much a part of the cultural fabric that it is taken for granted. Rock music blares out of car radios, computer speakers, and CD players from New York to Calcutta. Musicians who were famous during the baby boom era, such as Chuck Berry, Elvis Presley, the Beatles, Bob Dylan, Stevie Wonder, and thousands of others, changed the sound of music beyond reckoning.

As associate professor of history at the University of Michigan Douglas T. Miller and journalist Marion Nowak write, when rock first came along, it sent shock waves through society, alarming parents, politicians, and social critics. The idea of white suburban boys and girls dancing to African American rhythm and blues music was horrifying to many religious and civic leaders at a time of strict racial segregation. But for suburban teens repressed by society's rules, it was a breath of fresh air blowing through the otherwise conformist society of the 1950s.

In April 1955, *Life* magazine ran a massive pictorial article about a mysterious new "frenzied teenage music craze" that was creating "a big fuss." *Life* seemed rather confused by the new phenomenon, not sure whether to use its usual tone of buoyant approval, or that of more rarely summoned anger. The article, consequently, is an odd mixture of these two moods: at once indulgent (aren't these kids cute?) and disturbed (these kids are in trouble!). [Dance instructor] Arthur Murray, for instance, was quoted as saying rock and roll dancing was healthy for kids. But then there was the fact that the New Haven, Connecticut, police chief had banned all rock and roll parties, and "other towns are following suit."

Life went on, "some American parents, without quite know-ing what it is their kids are up to, are worried that its some-thing they shouldn't be."

By mid-decade, rock and roll was fast becoming teen-agers' music. This big change in musical habit rose out of several historical trends. One of the major factors was the al-tered state of teen-agers themselves. The widespread afflu-ence of the fifties shifted adolescent status. Middle-class white kids were simply expected to go to school and have lots of wholesome spare time. This new standard created a sense of separation among teen-agers. They were obviously too mature to be considered children. But then teens were too young to wield the power of adults. In the limbo of tran-sition and luxury, adolescents came to recognize themselves as unique, set apart, different. That perception marked the first throes of the developing postwar youth culture. . . .

Within Easy Reach

By 1950, the incredible rise of television was forcing radio into more music programming [as opposed to comedy, drama, and game shows]. At the same time, the mass migra-tion of blacks out of the rural South and into urban centers was increasing. Radio reflected this population movement with a surge of "race" programming, and so rhythm and blues came to the urban airwaves. Before the mid-forties, rhythm and blues music had been relatively inaccessible to whites. Race records were sold in ghetto stores, far removed from the experience of most white kids. By 1950, however, rhythm and blues was within easy reach of anyone. All a kid had to do was roll a dial.

The music scene as a whole, too, made it nearly inevitable that teens would take to some unique part of it. The musical market in the early fifties was based on careful demarcations. Each market appealed to the tastes of a certain group. Thus, one's tastes could easily indicate one's social class. There was "longhair"—that is, classical—music for highbrows (the ed-ucated); country and western for whites who were probably lower class, probably of rural background; jazz, the music of blacks and white aesthetes; the pop, "Hit Parade" ballads of the white middle class; and for city blacks there was rhythm and blues, the urban evolution of the blues. R & B, pop, and country music, as popular fields, all had their own separate charts rating a record's success.

Pop music, as the music of the white middle class, was sold to both teen-agers and their parents. No taste or social differences were acknowledged between young and old in the music's production. It was made to be mass-marketed. . . . Pop records had the final passionate impact of marshmallow whip. Look, for example, at the way one could express one's deepest emotions to a loved one: "If I Knew You Were Coming I'd've Baked a Cake" (a 1951 hit for Eileen Barton), or "Come On-a My House" ("I'm gonna give you candy . . ."), a hit for Rosemary Clooney in 1951. The songs spoke of yearning, longing, caring—of emotions reduced to cliché as substitutes for actual feelings. Similarly, they spoke in such euphemisms for sexual passion as the embrace or the one kiss that quenches desire. These phrases were certainly code words for sexual intercourse. But the code was so repressed, so deeply buried in the cultural subconscious, that most people could pretend it was not a code at all. Thus, the euphemisms were widely regarded as the reality. Any basic moving experience or raw feeling beneath the one ultimate kiss was treated as nonexistent. To mention the things that this age of artifice repressed was perceived as a dangerous and explosive act. It was also regarded as commercially impractical, a block against a record's reaching the top ten and [the popular TV show] "Your Hit Parade.". . .

There were . . . hints that pop music failed to satisfy the public. Many adults began to purchase records that were rather unique. The early fifties saw the rise of albums consisting purely of such sounds as racing car engines, jet-plane take-offs, cattle stampedes, or trains-in-tunnels. Millions of these records were sold in the decade. The taste for sheer noise, that is, was not the later creation of rock and roll. Perhaps the appeal of the sound-effects records rested in their strident attack on the enforced emotional stillness of those years.

Sometime in 1951, a disc jockey named Alan Freed was visiting a record store in downtown Cleveland. He was surprised to see white teen-agers buying rhythm and blues records, and even dancing to the music in the store. "I wondered," he recalled later, "I wondered for about a week. Then I went to the station manager and talked him into permitting me to follow my classical program with a rock 'n' roll party." These represented two of Freed's greatest contributions to the fluctuating music scene. First, he had made a name change, but an all-important one. Freed shrewdly recognized that the name "rhythm and blues" stigmatized that music. The fact of American racism condemned black tastes in general and so "race records" in particular. Freed redubbed it "rock and roll"—a ghetto euphemism for both dancing and sex. In titling his show "Moondog's Rock and Roll Party," Freed also legitimized the music in another way for white kids. Before, some whites already listened to all-black R & B radio shows. But it was not a taste cultivated by the mass of whites. Freed, as a white DJ, put the music in a more familiar and acceptable format, reassuring the majority of repressed and nervous white kids. His framework encouraged them to make the effort of overcoming their bland, stereotyped musical background. The R & B of Freed's early radio "party" was the strongest ancestor of the rock and roll that evolved a few years later.

Freed did more than begin playing black music for white audiences on the radio. Working in a medium that traditionally discriminated against black artists, Freed never forgot the R & B roots of rock, and always favored black performers on his shows. He entirely refused to play white cover versions of black songs. In 1957, Freed even banned all the recordings of [white teen idol] Pat Boone from his program. Freed also disseminated the music through other media. For instance, he presented black artists to largely white audiences with stage shows. In 1953, one such program at the Cleveland Arena was canceled because 30,000 people turned up to fight for the 10,000 seats. Two thirds of the crowd was white. The show was produced later that year, and included R & B stars Red Prysock, Joe Turner, Fats Domino, the Drifters, Ella Johnson, and the Moonglows. Freed's success in bringing black music to white audiences was frequently noted in [the music industry magazine] *Billboard*.

Between 1952 and 1954, the broadening taste that Freed had recognized began to affect the national music market. In 1952 the Clovers' "One Mint Julep" broke from the race category to sell on some white charts. Bill Haley and the Comets, a white ex-country group, pioneered a crude new style with "Crazy Man Crazy" in 1953. That same year the Orioles' "Crying in the Chapel," a race ballad, hit the white charts, as did "Money Honey" by the Drifters. . . .

To adults, these songs were all mysterious and somehow unpleasant. They were crude compared to the conventionalities of ballads. Only rarely did adults buy these records. It was growing clearer that, whatever else it might be, this music was for adolescents.

White Singers, Black Tunes

One of the most important things about these hits was that while the originals were performed by blacks, the best-sellers were recorded by whites. . . .

At the same time white singers were cleaning up on black tunes, another musical evolutionary step was being taken by Bill Haley and the Comets. Haley himself did some cleaned-up covers too. His version of "Shake, Rattle and Roll" significantly censored the lyrics of the Charles Calhoun tune originally sung by Joe Turner. Where Calhoun wrote "You wear low dresses, / The sun comes shinin' through," Haley revised the words to sing "You wear those dresses, / Your hair done up so nice." Haley also acquiesced to white sensibilities on stage, performing near-vaudeville tricks like playing the saxophone acrobatically. But the changes he imposed on such songs as "Shake, Rattle and Roll" represent an important aesthetic innovation. Haley's versions, unlike those of Boone . . . did not translate R & B into niceness. Nor were they straight imitations of the blues. What Haley did was to deliberately create a simple new formula for music, mixing up R & B with country. He took the basic African-originated beat and stripped away many musical effects—the loosely pronounced words, the complex and harmonious backing, the slurred note that is the blue note. He added some guitar work and other effects from "hillbilly" music. . . . In spite of the dishonesty of his censored lyrics, Haley recordings contained an emotional excitement that acted in opposition to most white cover versions. While those intended to reassure, to tone down the unfamiliar and scary elements of sex, beat, and feeling, Haley's thumping and shouting delivery was a powerful and liberating force for a white teen-age audience previously restricted to the pops.

Haley, of course, was only a musical transition point, too clumsy to last once his point became obvious. The synthesis of musical styles that he achieved increased into 1956. By that year, black artists were enjoying unprecedented successes selling to white audiences. In 1956, Little Richard's "Long Tall Sally" enjoyed its triumph. Adolescents came to purchase fully half the records pressed in America. And they bought black artists: Ray Charles, Little Richard, the Clovers, Chuck Berry ("Roll Over Beethoven"), Shirley and Lee ("Let the Good Times Roll"), the Five Satins ("In the Still of the Night"). All these performers had been impressed by the evolving musical scene. They all sang more lucidly, for instance, shunning the slurred pronunciation of blues tradition, to sell to whites as well as blacks. They also recognized the implications of crossing over. Chuck Berry originally intended "Maybellene" to be "Ida Mae," for the country market, and indeed it has both a blues-based beat and country-style guitar work. . . .

Elvis Changes Everything

Had Sam Phillips not discovered Elvis Presley in Memphis [in 1955], it would have been necessary to invent him. By mid-decade all the cultural groundwork had been laid for just such a star, doing just what he did to the music and the people. That is one reason for Elvis' incredibly rapid rise. By mid-decade, R & B was making the white charts. The record business, though, was showing persistent hostility toward black artists. It remained impossible for most white kids to conceive of a black singer as beloved idol. Music was also hovering on some transitory brink. Bill Haley had demonstrated that the mixing of various musical styles had prodigious impact. Elvis, then, took the music scene one step farther. He was not just mixing up country and ballads and blues. Nor did Elvis clean up the then outrageous parts of his act to sell. His manager, Colonel Tom Parker, created an Elvis image in shrewd conjunction with the times. Parker recognized the importance of facade. Elvis looked tough, brutal, confidently sensual. But he was, deep down, a good religious country boy, who loved his mother and his capitalist success and eventually went into the army with a patriotic smile. Elvis looked delinquent, but he was safe. And he was white, and so even safer. Presley's tremendous talent and charisma completed his success. Singing, Elvis was the convergence of all the pop traditions. He drew on the elaborate sentimentality of country. He had the pure floating voice of a balladeer; and he loved the rawness and the beat of the blues. All these elements appeared in his best fifties songs: the tough and derisive "Hound Dog," the desperate "Heartbreak Hotel," or the light yet urgent "Don't Be Cruel." But there was something more in his music. This was plainly a new musical form. It was not just a hack's tin pan alley synthesis but an evolutionary break.

One begins to get a feel for the sheer exciting newness of it all—of Elvis, of rock and roll—in looking at some statistics. Elvis was signed by RCA late in 1955. He recorded "Heartbreak Hotel." Within weeks it took the top position in both the pop and country charts, and was in the top five on the R & B chart. That this rapid rise and this crossing occurred was not completely unique. But Elvis continued to repeat that crosscultural success with a lengthy series of singles and albums. After six months, he had sold eight million records. In 1956, four of his singles in addition to "Heartbreak Hotel" sold amazingly. In the next two years, Elvis had a best-selling record during 55 of the 104 weeks. The record business had literally never known any single performer to achieve such consistent gigantic success. Nor had the business ever seen such numbers of ardent fans. Elvis quickly came to represent an utterly different sensibility to the music business and, indeed, to America at large.

Elvis was not the only rocker to make the charts, but he was the most outstanding of a vital and expanding field. He illustrates important things about changing musical tastes. The record producers had long assumed that R & B was somehow distasteful to white kids. This assumption entailed certain American bugaboos: fear and dislike of blacks, fear of explicit sex, fear of sensual experience and of autonomous expression. The crooners before Elvis had been like Perry Como, relaxed, muted, low-key in performance, or else limited belters like Eddie Fisher. Elvis was anything but muted or limited. On stage he celebrated all sorts of then-outrageous notions. He would ride on in a gold Cadillac, wearing a gold lamé suit. He would move any way he wanted. He would intersperse hit songs with gospel songs, tunes by country singers like Carl Perkins with R & B standards from Big Boy Crudup. Where a crooner such as Como or Al Martino might sing of tragic love in tones more suggesting apathy or drowsiness, Elvis delivered the real feeling. His immense emotional range, of course, received less publicity than his stage presence. As one rock critic has since written, "there was no more pretense about moonlight and hand-holding; it was hard physical fact."

It was also previously unheard of in the American mass market. Sexually explicit movements by a singer had been done before black audiences, or in sleazy bars or strip joints, but not before mainstream white America. . . .

A Middle-Class Nightmare

Adults, as the 1955 attitude of *Life* magazine indicated, had been unsure about just how to take to this new music. But by 1956, most adults knew: hostility was the rule. Elvis, as the king of rock, inevitably received much of the criticism. *Look* magazine's words seem to be a good metaphor for adult feelings toward the rock phenomenon as a whole. In an article entitled "He Can't Be—But He Is," the magazine moaned, "Presley is mostly nightmare." Consider the insular naivete and suspicion those quotes imply. Elvis, and by extension all his young fans, "can't be": there was no room for them in the mid-century conformity daydream. And so he could only be a "nightmare." Presley was a bad dream personified because this "vulgar" man, as *Look* wrote, this gyrating, leering, sensual star was popular. Popular with teen-agers. And not just the easily forgotten children of poor whites, of ghetto blacks, but with everyone's kids. No longer were the young mere extensions of their parents' musical tastes. Parents felt they were slipping out of control—if music was unfamiliar, what would be next?

Another *Look* article, talking about the Presley line of clothing and cosmetics, gratuitously injected an offhand comment that "the heavy divisions of the Presley force are half-grown females with half-baked ideas." That remark seems particularly strange considering the bulk of the article was puff for items like charm bracelets, sneakers, plaster of paris busts, and lipsticks (Hound Dog Orange, for instance). A Chicago radio station smashed Presley records on the air. Buffalo DJ Dick Biondi was fired for spinning Elvis records. A Cincinnati used-car dealer guaranteed to break fifty Presley records in the presence of every purchaser, and sold five cars in one day. Most animosity was directed toward the sensual implications of Elvis' act (and by extension, the implications of all rock and roll). But it was not just eroticism but self-expression in general that became the target of these angry adults. As *Look* magazine noted with disapproval, "When asked about the sex element in his act, he answers without blinking his big brown eyes, 'Ah don't see anything wrong with it. Ah just act the way Ah feel.'" Or, as New York *Times* reviewer Jack Gould commented after Elvis' famous Ed Sullivan [television show] appearance, "When Presley executes his bumps and grinds, it must be remembered by the Columbia Broadcasting System that even the 12-year-old's curiosity may be overstimulated."

Overstimulated? Half-baked? Nightmare? The adult reaction to Elvis, and even more to rock music in general, provides a brilliant counterpoint illuminating American ideas of freedom in the fifties. As such, it also shows how patterns of rebellion, of counterculture if you will, are provoked. Rock did coalesce teen-agers, did give them a feeling of being a unique social group with particular characteristics. And it did specify certain material urgencies—like the faddism of "Blue Suede Shoes" or, more usually, romantic emotions.

But there was no reason that any of this should have seemed politically revolutionary. . . .

In all this reaction one finds a single, central fear. The glowing core of that blurry fifties terror was a very real fear of autonomy and free expression. A quote from a book entitled *U.S.A. Confidential* is a good catchall of accusations against rock and roll. "Like a heathen religion, it is all tied up with tom-toms and hot jive and ritualistic orgies of erotic dancing, weed-smoking and mass mania, with African jungle background. Many music shops purvey dope; assignations are made in them. White girls are recruited for colored lovers. Another cog in the giant delinquency machine is the radio disc jockey. . . . We know that many platter-spinners are hop-heads. Many others are Reds, left-wingers, or hecklers of social convention. . . . Through disc jocks, kids get to know colored and other hit musicians; they frequent places the radio oracles plug, which is done with design . . . to hook juves and guarantee a new generation subservient to the Mafia." Nearly every phobia of American respectability at mid-century cropped up in exaggerated form in this paragraph. This, its authors insisted, was what rock and roll did to good white kids: it introduced them to their sexuality, to dope, to interracial contacts, to bizarre dance rituals involving the former; it taught them to distrust convention and finally it put them under Mafia rule. There are varying truths in all this. The Mafia accusation is dubious at best. Drugs were rarely part of the youth culture scene in the fifties—except for alcohol, a more acceptable vice. Probably rock's biggest contribution to racial equality was to economically enrich a few black artists—although white producers, southern white artists, and the cover singers really made the most money. . . .

Rock never really died. It is over two decades old and continues to explode all over the place. The affection for "oldies," itself interpreted as a sign of the weakness of the rock scene, is just a way of fondly remembering the history of rock on the part of those kids who themselves have so little history. For the young, by 1960, rock music was not dormant but managed to fulfill a number of functions. Some of these were contradictory. Even at its most furious the music had been unable to counter the life-programming most kids recognized as their future. Rock only provided a diversion from its colder constraints. But it was in the way rock and roll united teens as a self-acknowledged different group that the music performed its most challenging act: a challenge calling not for revolution but, more precisely, for reassessment. Once a teen-ager broke off from the music of adults, and especially once the parents began making bitter judgments about a simple matter of entertainment, a re-evaluation of more than the music was nearly inevitable. It was a re-evaluation refused, for the most part, until later years. But rock and roll did help contribute to a new attitude emerging in the late fifties. In that decade, America was a culture daydreaming of a false world, with Mr. Clean, Doris Day, General Ike, and universal luxury, without stress, Negroes, or genitalia. We were daydreaming, and rock was one of the forces that woke us up.

Chapter 2

The Rebellious Years

Turning Points

IN WORLD HISTORY

A Decade of Black Protest

Aldon D. Morris

African Americans experienced a postwar baby boom that resulted in increased enrollment in black colleges by the early sixties. And several years before white student protest rocked the country, the first wave of sixties sit-ins were organized by black students who demanded integrated lunch counters throughout the South. In the following excerpt Aldon D. Morris, professor of sociology and African American studies at the University of Michigan, explains that the protest techniques used by African Americans were imitated by white students who later went on to organize massive demonstrations against the Vietnam War.

Nineteen sixty was the year when thousands of Southern black students at black colleges joined forces with "old movement warriors" and tremendously increased the power of the developing civil rights movement. Between February 1 and April 1, 1960, students were involved in lunch counter sit-in demonstrations in approximately seventy Southern cities. It is significant that by 1960 Dr. [Martin Luther] King was only thirty-one years of age, and the average age of the top Southern Christian Leadership Council (SCLC) leaders was close to that. The youthfulness of those leaders suggested to black college students that they themselves should become more directly involved in the fight for their own liberation. Moreover, it was widely known in college circles that the courageous protesters in the Little Rock [Arkansas high school integration] crisis of 1957 were high school students. From the privileged position of hindsight, it is clear that the student sit-ins of 1960 were the introduction to a decade of political turbulence. . . .

Student sit-ins of 1960 rapidly evolved into a mass protest that strengthened the civil rights movement and its organizational base; gave rise to the Student Non-violent Coordinating Committee (SNCC), a major student civil rights organization; and gave rise to the modern white student movement of the early 1960s. The first step in explaining this complex set of phenomena is to investigate why black educational institutions and students were ideal candidates for involvement in the movement.

The term "black educational institutions" rather than "black colleges" is more fitting here, because elementary and high school, college, seminary, and university students were involved in the movement. Most of the analysis will focus on black colleges, however, because they were responsible for the bulk of the protest activities, but high school students also played an important role.

Black educational institutions were important to the movement because they, like the church, comprised organized groups with developed communication networks and skilled student leaders. Indeed, student governments, fraternities, sororities, kinship and friendship networks, and theological seminaries linked students, making the schools ideal organizations for rapid mobilization to occur. Several studies have shown that students who participated in the movement were more likely than nonparticipants to belong to these networks.

There was, however, an important difference between the schools and the churches. Most of the schools relied on financial support supplied by the white power structure. This meant that if the schools' administrations supported the movement their funds could be withdrawn. Dr. Mays, former president of Morehouse College stated the situation succinctly: "If you knew that the legislature, with no Negroes in at all, have got to decide on what you get, how you expect a bunch of radicalism coming out of that?" Rather than support the movement, therefore many of the teachers and administrators attempted to block it from taking root on the campuses.

Nevertheless, the schools housed a group relatively free of

those pressures—the students. Students are ideal candidates for protest activities. Usually they do not have families to support, employers' rules and dictates to follow, or crystallized notions of what is "impossible" and "unrealistic." Students have free time and boundless energy to pursue causes they consider worthwhile and imperative. But most of all, students were available for protest because, like the ministers, they were an organized group within the black community who were relatively independent of white economic control.

Most scholars of the 1960 sit-ins have consistently argued that they were a product of an independent student-initiated movement. But many of the students were in fact deeply involved with the movement centers already discussed here. This was inevitable given the historical close ties of black educational institutions with the churches. Indeed, many of the colleges were established by black churches. In many cases the churches that made up the movement centers had large student memberships and were referred to as college churches. . . .

In this analysis of the sit-in movement it will be demonstrated that the student sit-ins were rapidly spread by student leaders and leaders of the movement centers working in concert. It will be shown that in many instances it was the leaders of the movement centers who organized the student protesters. The tie between the students and the centers is crucial because of the atmosphere of intense repression in which the sit-ins spread. Without the mobilization of the black community by the centers, it is doubtful that the spread of the sit-ins could have been sustained.

The 1960 Student Sit-Ins

In the South during the 1950s segregation laws prohibited blacks and whites from eating together. In stores such as Woolworth's and Kresge's Southern blacks could shop but could not eat at the segregated lunch counters. On February 1, 1960, four black freshmen students at North Carolina Agricultural and Technical College in Greensboro violated the law by taking seats at the segregated lunch counter of the local Woolworth store and asked to be served. Within weeks similar sit-ins were rapidly spreading across the South. Between February 1 and March 1, 1960, sit-in protests had occurred at segregated lunch counters in eleven cities in North Carolina; seven in Virginia; four in South Carolina; three in Florida; two in Tennessee; two in Alabama; one in Kentucky; and one in Maryland. In the month of March sit-ins continued to spread within these states, and by the end of the month they had spread to cities in Georgia, Texas, Ohio, West Virginia, Louisiana, and Arkansas. . . .

The dramatic sit-ins and the emergence of SNCC had an immediate national impact. Activist-oriented students at predominantly white Northern campuses were instantly struck by the sit-ins' rapid spread across the South and by the fact that most of the black demonstrators were college students. [Author] Kirkpatrick Sale captured the response of these students to the sit-ins:

[B]y the end of that spring students at perhaps a hundred Northern [white] colleges had been mobilized in support, and over the next year civil-rights activity touched almost every campus in the country: support groups formed, fund raising committees were established, local sit-ins and pickets

After being denied service at a whites-only lunch counter, a group of black college students stage a sit-in protest at a Woolworth store in Greensboro, North Carolina.

took place, campus civil-rights clubs began, students from around the country traveled to the South.

No previous actions of the Southern civil rights movement had generated this kind of widespread activism among whites across the nation. In effect, the 1960 sit-ins generated the activist stage of the modern white student movement. The central question is, Why did the sit-ins have this effect?

Effects on Young, White Students

To get at the answer, it is instructive to know what type of white students usually became involved in the movement during the sit-ins. Studies have shown that the typical student was affluent, excelled in scholarly pursuits, usually majored in the social sciences, and had liberal-to-radical political values. Thus the students were not marginal to universities, but they were dissatisfied with the huge gap between America's democratic rhetoric and its actual practices. But prior to the sit-ins these students were likely to engage in academic analysis of social problems and debate them at student government meetings rather than attempt to change them through overt protest and demonstrations. The black student sit-ins challenged that approach. In the words of one activist of the period, "the sit-ins demonstrated that white students could act on their beliefs rather than sitting on them."

We can begin to answer the question of why that discontented group of affluent white students became involved in the politics of protest. That group entered into the politics of protest because the sit-ins by dominated black students provided them with a visible protest model, which demonstrated how they could proceed tactically and organizationally. It was an especially attractive model because the white student shared two important characteristics with the sit-in demonstrators: Both groups were students, and both were young.

Direct action became the tactic of the emerging white student movement, and SNCC supplied the organizational blueprint. There was no denying that the sit-ins were direct action. They demonstrated to white students that youth could enter the political process directly and force older generations to yield to their demands. White student leaders quickly realized that the methods of direct action allowed them to take the initiative away from adult authorities and to formulate their own policy. Direct action techniques, according to one activist and scholar of the period, "were seen by white intellectual students as ways of living one's values and simultaneously changing the world." Beginning in early 1960, such pioneering white student leaders as Robert Haber and Tom Hayden of the University of Michigan adopted the method of nonviolent direct action and spent considerable time at civil rights conferences and workshops with black activists, who taught them how to apply it.

Students for a Democratic Society (SDS), the chief white student movement organization of the 1960s, was modeled after SNCC. White student activists were impressed that black students involved in the sit-ins organized their own independent organization. In January 1960 SDS was a small student organization with little visibility. Following the sit-ins representatives of SDS went south and observed the meetings from which SNCC was organized. [SNCC member] Ella Baker's philosophy on leadership and organizational structure was adopted by leaders of SDS. Obviously influenced by SNCC, Robert Haber, the most central figure in organizing SDS, contended:

> SDS should play down the . . . idea of establishing its own little chapters for its own little purposes at various campuses and concentrate instead on forming alliances with the existing campus groups that had already come into being in response to their own local needs. . . . Second . . . SDS could play its most valuable role by trying to coordinate these groups and service their needs on a national scale. . . . Third, SDS should involve itself as much as possible with direct social action.

Clearly, these were the same ideas articulated by Baker, which shaped and molded SNCC. Haber attended some of the early SNCC meetings, and he acknowledges that they had an important impact on him. Shortly after SNCC was organized, Haber served as liaison between SNCC and SDS. That function allowed him to attend top-level meetings of

SNCC. During this period, Haber recalls, Ella Baker provided a bridge between the black student movement and the emerging white student movement. SDS, like SNCC, emerged as a loosely structured organization that emphasized local autonomy and direct action rather than strong centralized leadership. In this sense Ella Baker was the "mother" of both SNCC and the activist phase of SDS.

Overall I have argued that the activist stage of the modern white student movement was generated by the 1960 sit-ins, because they provided these students with a protest model with both a tactical and an organizational blueprint. In short, from an indigenous perspective it is expected that dissatisfied members of affluent groups will enter into protest following a suitable tactical innovation made possible by well-developed movement centers of a dominated group. The sit-ins also provided a favorable climate for the further development of the SCLC.

The Roots of Student Rebellion

Terry H. Anderson

The sixties and early seventies are remembered as a time of student protest and rebellion. Between 1964 and 1973, student demonstrations accelerated from peaceful sit-ins to bloody confrontations with police and National Guard troops. In the following excerpt, professor of history at Texas A&M University and Vietnam veteran Terry H. Anderson writes about the first protests and explains how sixties American culture acted as a breeding ground for student rebellion.

"Last summer I went to Mississippi to join the struggle there for civil rights," said Berkeley student Mario Savio in 1964. "This fall I am engaged in another phase of the same struggle, this time in Berkeley. In Mississippi an autocratic and powerful minority rules, through organized violence, to suppress the vast, virtually powerless majority. In California, the privileged minority manipulates the university bureaucracy to suppress the students' political expression."

That expression had been curtailed by the University of California as students arrived on the Berkeley campus for fall semester in September. As was typical for university officials during the cold war era, a dean simply informed all student organizations that from now on they were no longer permitted to set up tables on campus to promote "off-campus" causes such as civil rights, and this ban applied to the traditional area for such endeavors, a small strip of property at the campus's main entrance where Telegraph Avenue met Bancroft Way. . . .

By the 1963–64 academic year hundreds of students had become involved in civil rights demonstrations, picketing

From *The Movement and the Sixties*, by Terry H. Anderson. Copyright © 1996 by Terry H. Anderson. Used by permission of Oxford University Press, Inc.

hotels, automobile dealerships, restaurants, and other businesses that had discriminatory employment practices. At Lucky food stores, activists held "shop-ins," filling grocery carts with food, and after going through the checkout line, saying, "Sorry, I forgot my money. If you would hire some Negroes I would remember it next time." They picketed the Oakland *Tribune*, whose conservative owner was on the university's board of regents, and in March the local campaign reached a crescendo when 2000 violated a court order restricting the number of protesters in front of the Sheraton Palace Hotel; police arrested 800.

Political debate also was mounting. The Republican convention was held during June 1964 in San Francisco and the candidacy of conservative Barry Goldwater inspired discussion as he faced Lyndon Johnson in the upcoming elections. Then, in August, just weeks before students returned to classes, President Johnson declared that North Vietnam had attacked U.S. ships in the Gulf of Tonkin. He asked for and received from Congress the Gulf of Tonkin Resolution, which [drastically increased U.S. involvement in Vietnam and] stimulated more student debate about America's role in South Vietnam. And as fall semester began in September approximately fifty students returned from volunteer [civil rights] work [in Mississippi]. At Berkeley and at other universities many of these students were welcomed back to campus as "civil rights heroes."

The university administration apparently was under pressure by conservatives in the state, community, and on the board of regents to curb activism when they issued the political ban. The students' response was dramatic. On September 21 campus organizations of all political persuasions united . . . and they violated the ban. Two hundred students picketed on campus with signs such as "UC Manufactures Safe Minds," "Ban Political Birth Control," and "Bomb the Ban." To most, the issue was freedom of speech. "We're allowed to say why we think something is good or bad," said activist Jackie Goldberg, "but we're not allowed to distribute information as to what to do about it. . . . The movement gained support, and a week later some students set up political tables. Administrators took down names, and ordered civil rights veteran Jack Weinberg to appear in front of a dean. He did the next day, but he was followed by 900 supporters who packed into the administration building, Sproul Hall, and stayed until early the next morning. University of California president Clark Kerr suspended eight activists, but that did not stifle dissent as it would have in the 1950s. It only increased ill will and resulted in more protest. "A student who has been chased by the KKK in Mississippi," said student Roger Sandall, "is not easily seared by academic bureaucrats."

The Free Speech Movement it was called, and along with the civil rights protests the previous spring it demonstrated the emergence of a new generation. "How proud I felt," wrote Berkeley student Sara Davidson. "I belonged to a great new body of students who cared about the problems of the world. No longer would youth be apathetic. That was the fifties. We were *committed.*"

Ever since, Berkeley has been synonymous with student protest and campus rebellion in the 1960s. Historians have

In 1964 hundreds of students at the University of California's Berkeley campus spent the night in Sproul Hall, following a sit-in protest against the university's restriction on political activities.

described the rise of student power by examining the events at Berkeley in 1964 and then those at Columbia University in 1968 as if little happened during those years on other campuses. Sociologists and psychologists have written a library of articles and books postulating numerous theories of why students were challenging the system—family affluence, permissive child rearing, developmental stress, the impending collapse of capitalism, and even that young male students were plagued with castration complexes. These interpretations are misleading. During the mid-1960s the rise of student power was a national phenomenon concerning many more issues than just free speech on one prominent campus. Furthermore, social science theories might explain the behavior of some individuals, but will not account for the rise of campus turmoil. Instead, one must examine the massive new generation—the sixties generation—as a sizable percentage arrived on campuses, and then discovered that university administrators restricted their personal behavior and constitutional rights.

The Sixties Generation

In 1964 and 1965 the first babies born after World War II were coming of age; they were celebrating their eighteenth birthdays. The enormous postwar birth rate lasted eighteen years, from 1946 to 1964, and it resulted in the largest generation in our history, over 70 million, the baby boomers. Their sheer numbers changed the face of the nation. In 1960, because of the low birth rate during depression and war, America had grown middle-aged; there were only 16 million youths, 18- to 24-year-olds. The baby boom, however, brought about a dramatic shift. By 1970, the number of youth soared to about 25 million. Suddenly, the nation was young. The "sixties generation" included baby boomers who were born in the late 1940s and early 1950s, and the generation also comprised older siblings, those born during World War II who became the "first wave" of activists in the early 1960s. Consequently the sixties generation could be defined to include anyone who turned eighteen during the era from 1960 to 1972. The oldest was born in 1942 and turned 30 in 1972, and the youngest was born in 1954 and turned 18 in 1972. This generation numbered over 45 million, about 33 million who also were part of the baby boom, and this group felt special, especially after the traumatic events of the decade. A 1969 survey revealed that 80 percent of youth felt part of "my generation."

America seemed young, and in mid-decade being part of the sixties generation was suddenly important. Businesses cashed in on youth as Ford Motor Company developed a car for kids, the Mustang, and as a soft drink company proclaimed the arrival of the "Pepsi Generation." To explain, exploit, or cater to the young became an obsession, and the number of commercials soared while articles on youth tripled during the decade. The Associated Press declared that youth "made more headlines than anybody. . . . 1964 would have to go down as the Year of the Kids." In 1965 *Newsweek* claimed that "America's future has always belonged to its youth but never before have the young staked out so large a claim to America's present." And *Time* proclaimed, "For the Man of the Year 1966 is a generation: the man—and woman—of 25 and under."

Furthermore, and because of postwar affluence, the sixties generation had an opportunity missed by their parents' depression generation. The children could spend years at college, even travel, before they "had to settle down." This increased the probability of a "generation gap" between parents and kids. The years between the late teens and early twenties usually are stressful, rebellious, as individuals search for themselves, a mate, a career. The decade was destined to be more rambunctious than earlier eras as baby boomers passed through growing pains. The large number of kids also meant that throughout the decade there always would be an abundant supply of young faces entering college, being drafted, or being examined by academics and journalists.

Yet in the mid-1960s what it meant to be part of the sixties generation was uncertain. Journalists labeled some youth "committed," but they named most the "explosive," "aloof" and especially the "cool" generation. Taking the term from jazz and the beatniks, the media declared that this generation felt that it was "cool" to be young.

The nation seemed flooded with the cool generation, and they began exhibiting youthful forms of rebellion as they dominated the American scene. Spring breaks at Fort Lauderdale became an annual pilgrimage for boys participating in the great hunt for "beach, broads and booze," while at Daytona Beach they searched for "sex, sand, suds and sun." On Easter weekend some 75,000 collegians held a huge bash at Daytona Beach. All was rather serene until one girl, who was being tossed on a blanket, lost her swimsuit. The riot was on. A Michigan State sophomore boasted, "I just came to have me some fun and get drunk," as police arrested almost 2000 for public promiscuity and drinking.

Labor Day weekend the party moved to Hampton Beach, New Hampshire. Some 10,000 teens arrived at the quiet seashore resort which prohibited beer and the new fad, "bundling," sleeping together on the beach. Kids naturally broke the law and a riot ensued. Police attempted to disperse the crowd with fire hoses, tear gas and dogs, but eventually the governor had to call in the National Guard. The ruckus lasted two nights, and the authorities drove the crowd three miles, literally across the state line and into Massachusetts. Those who did not get out of town were arrested, and the judge showed the older generations' displeasure by handing out stiff sentences of up to nine months in jail and $1000 fines. While the governor stated that the beach riot was a "symptom of the moral sickness in American youth," the kids disagreed. To many in the sixties generation, the decade was becoming one long party.

Meanwhile in California: Surf's Up! Golden girls and flexing boys apparently surfed an endless wave or played a continual game of volleyball before pizzas, nightly parties, and some heavy panting. Young love was celebrated in numerous movies between 1963 and 1965: *Beach Party, Muscle Beach Party, Bikini Beach, Beach Blanket Bingo.* By all appearances, the girls and guys of the "Mickey Mouse Club" had graduated from the show and were having a wonderful time, wiggling and giggling, bulging out of their swimsuits. It appeared that everyone was eager to learn "How to Stuff a

Wild Bikini." As The Beach Boys sang "Surfin U.S.A." and drove their "Little Deuce Coupe," tanned "California Girls" exclaimed, "Life's so bitchin'!"

A Sexual Revolution

It was more than that, for the sixties generation was getting its first taste of the sexual revolution. Birth control pills became available for married women, and by mid-decade single coeds were flocking to family planning clinics, wearing a friend's wedding ring, and getting their monthly prescriptions of "the pill." Along with the diaphragm, the pill dramatically increased a woman's feeling of independence as it placed birth control in her hands and liberated her from the dreaded fear of getting pregnant. The press began writing about sexual mores of the young, and *Newsweek* explained to the older generation the new definition of a "technical virgin," a "boy or girl who has experienced almost all varieties of heterosexual sex—except intercourse."

Men made new demands on their girlfriends, turning up the pressure to "do it." A "boy used to date two girls simultaneously, a nice girl and a not-so-nice girl," a Michigan coed explained. "Now he wants two girls in one. The nice girl who doesn't want to go along has a problem." A Bennington female stated, "If a girl reaches 20 and she's still a virgin, she begins to wonder whether there's anything wrong with her," and a Vassar coed added, "It's a load off my mind, losing my virginity."

The older generation was shocked. "Morals don't mean a thing to them," a beach hotel manager said about the kids during spring break in Florida. In Darien, Connecticut, a suburban community that prided itself on wholesome children, church attendance, and propriety, parents were alarmed by reports of high school pregnancies, heavy drinking, and "sexual activity going on at the drive-in-theater of every kind and degree."

The kids were beginning to express values of their own generation. "We've discarded the idea that the loss of virginity is related to degeneracy," an Ohio State senior explained. "Premarital sex doesn't mean the down fall of society, at least not the kind of society that we're going to build."

That society was becoming increasingly sexy as the sixties generation dominated the media. In fashion, the girls of the 1950s had grown out of their bobby sox and pedal-pushers and in 1964 began wearing mini-skirts. Hemlines never had revealed so much leg, and many older women quickly adopted the new fad, even Jackie Kennedy. Coeds, meanwhile, were taking off one-piece bathing suits and wearing smaller and smaller "itsy bitsy teenie weenie yellow polka dot" bikinis, while some models created a sensation by wearing topless swimsuits. Teenagers bought what parents called "a dirty

Haight-Ashbury Tourist Advice

The psychedelic San Francisco hippie social experiment quickly captured America's attention. Before long, thousands of tourists were streaming into the Haight-Ashbury neighborhood to look at the "freaks"—and maybe join in the fun. To counter the invasion of the "straights" an underground newspaper called the Haight-Ashbury Maverick, *printed up a tongue-in-cheek brochure to give advice to thrill-seeking sightseers visiting hippie central.*

Many tourists upon seeing the unshaven, unconventionally clothed Love Generation roll up their car windows and lock the doors. This is not necessary and can be mightily inconvenient. Some of the hippies do bite, but all of them have taken their rabies shots so their bite is not too bad. Honestly though, you must consider that the unconventional attire would make it easy to describe your assailant to the police. By the way, if it appears to you that there are no police in the area, have no fears— probably one out of every twenty males that you see between the ages of 25 and 35 is an [undercover] officer of some kind or the other. . . .

Then there are the Flower Children. . . . These are the most lovable of all the hippies. Early in the summer it was quite common to have them going down the streets passing out flowers and wearing garlands of flowers. But flowers are rather expensive to come by, and even a small bunch of flowers is getting be-

magazine," *Playboy*. Hugh Hefner's sexual values were merged with the 1950s can-do masculinity and presented on film in numerous James Bond movies. Sean Connery became the John Wayne to the sixties generation as he merged technology and sex to pursue "Pussy Galore" in *Goldfinger*.

Influence of the Beatles

"Most of all," the Associated Press wrote about 1964, "it was the year of the Beatles." The Beatles did not just come to America; they invaded. In February the rock group arrived at Kennedy International Airport and were met by 3000

---

yond the reach of those of moderate (or less) means.

Then there are the bikeriders. When you see them on the street, they just plain look rough. And they damn well can be, But since they want the right to live their own life—as they choose—they respect the right of the others to do likewise. And they might well be the ones who defend in acts the rights of those who are unprepared to do so. The riders primarily keep to a certain area but mix well in all the other areas of Haight Street.

And there are many many other tribes of hippies. . . .

If you have come to the Haight looking for grass, then we suggest that you give up that long drive for these six blocks. There just isn't any around. Acid is also very scarce. Most tourists assume that they can pick up some for their private uses back in Oshkosh and Dallas. Sorry, it is just not so. Besides every nark (narcotics agent) in California is here, and if there is any grass about, it will be in their hands shortly. We strongly urge, however, that you might be able to get some in your home town, and we further strongly urge that you smoke a joint before retiring and throw away those patent-medicine Nytol, Sleepeze, and so forth. Grass is so much better for relaxing. Try it instead of that martini before dinner; be sure, be safe, and use pot instead of gin.

Irwin Unger and Debi Unger, eds., *The Times Were a Changin': The Sixties Reader*. New York: Three Rivers Press, 1998. Originally printed in the *Haight-Ashbury Maverick*, August 1967.

screaming fans, mostly teenage girls. The Fabulous Four could not get through the crowd without the help of 200 policemen. For a month the group performed to shrieking, squealing audiences, and when they made their American TV debut on the Ed Sullivan Show, the program received the highest ratings in history: 72 percent of the New York audience tuned in. Beatlemania was an instant fad, and soon many of the sixties generation were abandoning crew cuts for long bangs and black boots.

The Beatles' sound and lyrics were similar to American popular music at that time; it was as adolescent as the baby boomers. Top hits of the era included Leslie Gore whining "It's my party and I'll cry if I want to," the Angels sneering, "My Boyfriend's back and you're gonna be in trouble," the Kingsmen slurring, "Louie, Louie," or the Temptations talking about "My Girl," my girl. Most popular, however, were surfer groups such as Jan and Dean and the Beach Boys, or the Motown sound of the Supremes. Between summer 1963 and 1965 the Beach Boys had nine songs in the top ten and the themes were "I Get Around," "Surfer Girl," and "Do You Wanna Dance." While Jan and Dean were squealing around "Dead Man's Curve" en route to "Surf City," the Supremes sang "Baby Love" and wondered "Where Did Our Love Go?" The Beatles had the answer: "I Want to Hold Your Hand," "All My Loving," "And I Love Her." If it was "A Hard Day's Night" for the Beatles, it was not for the Beach Boys, who just had "Fun, Fun, Fun," telling the generation to "Dance, Dance, Dance." Kids agreed, and performed what one reporter labeled, "touch-less, wildly tribalistic dances like the 'frug' and the 'swim' and the 'mashed potato.'" Everyone was having "good, goood, gooood, good vibrations."

Yet the Beatles were having more impact than other bands. They were part of the British Invasion which included many English bands and which demonstrated that rock and roll—although a uniquely American invention—was becoming the music of the international postwar baby boom: The sixties would not just be an American phenomenon. Also, the Beatles looked and acted differently than clean-cut American performers. After the crew-cut 1950s, the "Fab Four" had relatively long, shaggy hair. After an era of learning "to respect your elders," they seemed irreverent, even joking about the Queen of England. The Beatles movie in 1965, *A Hard Day's Night*, was "almost all joy," a student critic wrote, because "all the dreary old adults are mocked and brushed aside." To many young Americans, these musicians symbolized rejection of 1950s morality, a revolt against authority, and estrangement from parents. "My mother hates them, my father hates them, my teacher hates them," said a young fan. "Can you think of three better reasons why I love them?"

A subtle revolt was under way, a generational conflict in which many youth felt different from their parents. As adolescents sprouted into adulthood they realized that their values were unique; they were more idealistic and tolerant, less concerned with Communism. A third of these high school graduates headed off to college, three times the percentage as during their parents' generation, and that naturally began to create tensions between moms and dads and their collegiate sons and daughters. "We sent them to a university," parents would say, "that's more than we ever had. What more could they want?" The generation gap was becoming evident by 1965, and The Who expressed it in song:

> People try to put us down,
> just because we get around,
> Things they do look awful cold
> I hope I die before I get old. . . .
> Why don't you all fade away
> Don't try to dig what we all say.

That alienation naturally appeared on campus. *Newsweek* noted, "The young successfully 'Beatle-ized' the nation, and many think they may be about to 'Berkeley-ize' it as well."

The Folk Music Message

On campuses and in coffeehouses a growing number of students had been listening to young folk singers declaring the dawn of a new era. The cover blurb on Peter, Paul and Mary's debut album in 1962 proclaimed that the record "is bright with enthusiasm. No gimmicks. There is just something *Good* about it all. . . . One thing is for sure in any case: Honesty is back. Tell your neighbor." Many did, and soon the generation was singing out with Phil Ochs, Joan Baez, Tom Paxton, Judy Collins, Leonard Cohen, the Chad Mitchell Trio, and the Brothers Four.

The folk musicians' message was popular; it stated the emerging values of the sixties generation. ABC began a show in 1963 that featured folk singers, "Hootenanny," and soon ten million watched each week. At the same time Bob Dylan produced *The Freewheelin' Bob Dylan*, which sold 200,000 copies in two months, a remarkable number then for a folksinger. The album featured the first popular protest song about the military-industrial complex, "Masters of War,' and one about nuclear apocalypse, "A Hard Rain's a Gonna Fall," and it questioned the older generation in "Blowin' in the Wind." Later that year Peter, Paul and Mary released a single of "Blowin' in the Wind" and it sold over 300,000 copies in less than two weeks, eventually over a million, making it the first protest song to make the hit parade.

Many folk songs concerned the most important issue of the day in the first half of the 1960s—civil rights. The Chad Mitchell Trio sang a satiric tune about segregation at the University of Mississippi entitled "Alma Mater"; Tom Paxton skewered segregationists in his "Dogs of Alabama"; and Phil Ochs decried the southern way of life in "Talking Birmingham Jam" and "Here's to the State of Mississippi." Peter, Paul and Mary sang "If I Had a Hammer," proclaiming that they did have a hammer, a bell, and a song: "It's the hammer of Justice, it's the bell of freedom, It's the song about love between my brothers and my sisters, all over this land." And in "Blowin' in the Wind" Dylan posed a moral choice to his generation:

> How many roads must a man walk, before you call him a man?
> Yes, 'n' how many times can a man turn his head
> Pretending he just doesn't see?
> The answer my friend is blowin' in the wind,
> The answer is blowin' in the wind.

"The first way to answer these questions," said Dylan, "is by asking them. . . . I still say that some of the biggest criminals are those that turn their heads away when they see wrong and know it's wrong." Folksingers felt a warm wind of change blowing from the southern struggle, a breeze carrying new values, and in 1965 Dylan warned mothers and fathers:

> Your sons and your daughters are beyond your command
> Your old road is rapidly aging.
> Please get out of the new one
> If you can't lend a hand
> For the times they are a' changin'

Flooding the Classrooms

Times were changing on campus as the first baby boomers began flooding classrooms in mid-decade. In the past, higher education had been reserved for wealthy Americans usually enrolled in private colleges. Before World War II more students attended private than public institutions, but that changed after the conflict. The government awarded veterans the GI Bill, which paid their tuition; a strong post-war economy meant that many more families could help their children enroll in state universities; and then, in 1957, the Soviets challenged America—the Russians launched [the first earth-orbiting satellite] Sputnik. The race for space was on! Parents in the suburbs began wondering if [the Soviet] Little Ivan was smarter than [the American] Little Terry. Congress responded by passing the National Defense Education Act, which granted scholarships and some loans to science and engineering students, and in 1965 President Johnson dramatically enlarged the student loan program as part of his Great Society [social welfare program].

Education had been democratized. If the mind was willing, virtually anyone could enroll at a university. "Of course I went to college," said a baby boomer. "That was assumed." By the end of the 1960s three-quarters of university students were enrolled at public institutions and almost half of all kids 18 to 21 were attending college. Enrollments soared. In 1960 there were three million college students, but in autumn 1964 the first baby boomers hit campus and by the next year there were five million and that doubled to ten million by 1973. This meant the rise of a new form of higher education, the large public university. Before World War II there was not one university with over 15,000 students, yet by 1970 over fifty institutions had that enrollment and eight campuses were stuffed with over 30,000. . . .

The sixties generation began to confront its university administrations in 1964, politely demanding to be heard. During spring semester the administration at Brandeis consulted no one and then instituted new, stricter dorm visitation rules. That prompted several hundred students to stage a two-day demonstration, and the campus newspaper declared that such regulations "makes impossible any meaningful relationship between boy and girl." That fall semester, Syracuse University students approached their administrators with a simple request—they felt that holiday break, which began on December 23, was too close to Christmas. A few dozen students asked for more travel time to get home by Christmas Eve. After officials turned down all petitions, the students called a rally in December, and they were surprised when 2000 appeared. They demanded a speech from the chancellor, and he gave a short address, again saying no. As he ended his talk, some students jeered and booed, which shocked elders. "The students were supposed to show proper respect," a journalist wrote, "to know their place and keep it." Student activists, however, had a different interpretation. They wanted some role in the university. "If today's demonstration proves nothing else," the student paper editorialized, "we are not ones to be ignored or taken lightly."

Students at Berkeley certainly were not going to be taken lightly—they again challenged the ban on disseminating literature. On October 1, Jack Weinberg and others set up a few tables outside the administration building on Sproul Plaza and began passing out civil rights and political flyers. Before noon two university deans and a policeman approached Weinberg. "Are you prepared to remove yourself and the table from university property?" asked the dean. "I am not," replied Weinberg. After a brief discussion the official informed Weinberg of his arrest, and at this point several hundred students who were gathering for a free speech rally startled the officials by shouting, "Take us all, take us all!" Policemen drove a car onto the plaza and placed Weinberg inside, but suddenly someone shouted, "Sit down!" "I'm around the police car," recalled [protester] Michael Rossman. "I'm the first person to sit down. You will hear five hundred others who say that, and everyone is telling the truth." Students either laid or sat down around the car. They refused to move. The police could not drive their prisoner to jail as the crowd swelled to 3000. Mario Savio and many others climbed on top of the car and gave speeches, and later the crowd sang civil rights songs. They remained on the plaza all night. The next morning the area looked like a campsite, filled with sleeping bags, blankets, and even a pup tent. The crowd increased to 4000 that afternoon and President Kerr realized that the free speech issue was not going to disappear. After a thirty-hour sit-in, university administrators finally agreed to meet the activists.

To university officials, and to most citizens after the law and order 1950s, Berkeley had been reduced to chaos. Although campus rebellion would become common later in the decade, this was the first major eruption, and administrators responded forcefully. Under pressure from conservatives in the community and state government, they allowed 500 police officers to appear on campus minutes before they met activists. The police were armed with nightsticks, and the sight shocked students who never could remember a police army on campus and who felt that the incident was novel in American educational history. As police stood by, civil rights veterans taught nonviolent arrest tactics and urged those with police records or children to leave. Administrators had the support of California Governor Edmund G. Brown, a Democrat who stated that the demonstration was "not a matter of freedom of speech" but was an attempt by the students to use the campus illegally. "This will not be tolerated." He continued, "We must have—and will continue to have—law and order on our campuses."

Negotiations with Kerr continued for two hours, and

then Savio and other students emerged from Sproul Hall. Savio climbed on the police car and announced that an agreement had been reached. A student-faculty committee would examine the free speech issue and make recommendations to the president. The university would not press charges against Weinberg or FSM leaders, and the eight students suspended earlier would have their case reviewed. Kerr seemed to support establishing a small free speech area at the campus's main entrance where Telegraph Avenue met Bancroft Way.

Dropping Out of Society

Timothy Miller

The hippie movement that swept across America in the 1960s was one of the greatest cultural revolutions in history. Never before had so many middle-class children so thoroughly rejected the values of their parents. After experimenting with marijuana and psychedelic drugs such as LSD, young adults who had grown up in strict conformity in sanitized suburbs quickly began to question the religious, social, cultural, and political values of the older generation. As Timothy Miller, assistant professor of religious studies at the University of Kansas explains, many in the counterculture movement were convinced that they could create an entirely new society based on peace, love, and drug-induced mind expansion.

The counterculture was a romantic social movement of the late 1960s and very early 1970s, mainly composed of teenagers and persons in their early twenties, who through their flamboyant lifestyle expressed their alienation from mainstream American life. *Counterculture*, written as one word or two, became the standard term for the movement (or nonmovement, as some would have it) after the appearance, in 1969, of Theodore Roszak's influential book *The Making of a Counter Culture*. Until then, several competing terms described the cultural revolt of the young; other early contenders were *alternative culture* and *the underground*.

Any culture, of course, can spawn its countercultures, and thus the hippies were part of a long tradition of cultural demurring. In many ways their most obvious and immediate predecessors were the bohemians and beatniks who inhabited earlier decades of the twentieth century. The progression from beat to hip is a fairly obvious one; the beats of the 1950s advocated dropping out of society, promoted new forms of art and literature, smoked marijuana, listened to unorthodox music (jazz), rejected traditional sexual norms, and even popularized the word "hip.". . .

Behind both the 1960s counterculture and its predecessor beat culture lay black America. Although the hippies were mainly white (more about that later), they were cultural outsiders, renegades who deviated from the American Way of Life. Black radicals (Malcolm X, W.E.B. duBois) were countercultural heroes because they refused to compromise with the white and prosperous Establishment. Black musicians gave heart as well as soul to hip music. (Bob Dylan and the Beatles may have been the principal cultural icons, but the energy of Chuck Berry and Little Richard wrote the grammar of rock.) Black musicians were smoking marijuana decades before white dropouts had heard of it. [Best-selling author] Norman Mailer was writing about beatniks in his 1957 essay "The White Negro," but his observations apply equally to hippies:

It is no accident that the source of Hip is the Negro for he has been living on the margin between totalitarianism and democracy for two centuries. But the presence of Hip as a working philosophy in the sub-philosophies of American life is probably due to jazz. . . . In this wedding of the white and the black it was the Negro who brought the cultural dowry. Any Negro who wishes to live must live with danger from his first day.

And, Mailer concluded, even the jargon of hip was shaped in major part by "the Negro jazzman who was the cultural mentor of a people."

Declaration of Evolution

The counterculture's participants, usually called hippies, found themselves cast adrift from the prevailing values of society and tried, variously, to effect major changes in majority society or to drop out of it. As the hippies saw things, the Establishment—the tired, entrenched, declining dominant system—was rotten to the core, and a new society needed to arise on the cultural dunghill. Some hippies were escapists who simply favored withdrawal from the prevailing culture; others proposed much more active opposition to and confrontation with it as a necessary step on the road to cultural freedom and progress.

The counterculture had a vocal separatist minority which rejected the dominant culture wholesale and proclaimed the necessity of creating a new, independent, egalitarian society, although the means for getting there were usually murky. Separatist rhetoric could be powerful: one notable separatist document, "The Declaration of Cultural Evolution," written in 1968 by a committee including [counterculture icons] Timothy Leary, Allen Ginsberg, Paul Krassner, and Abbie Hoffman, listed, in a style imitative of the Declaration of Independence, grievances against majoritarian society—political repression, destruction of the environment, war, and the like. The Declaration maintained that the counterculture had pointed the way to needed social changes, but that "many have been deaf to the voice of reason.". . . Therefore, "human beings everywhere are, and quite properly ought to be, absolved from all allegiance to the present Cultural Arrangements insofar as they are obsolete and harmful."

Similarly another early theoretician of hip, Art Johnston, denounced the "Ethic of the Cool" in the West, which he defined as conformity to the status quo, the only goal of which was getting a good return on one's investment. He wrote that since it was very difficult to live outside the existing system, the function of the counterculture was defiance of the dominant mores. The counterculture was rebellion, a living protest vote, a declaration of choice—the Great Refusal to cooperate.

Still another separatist, Jean-Jacques Lebel, wrote . . . of a "containment industry" that aimed to pacify and neutralize the American young. It operated by separating art from life (that is, by having professional artists who displaced popular spontaneous art), by advancing symbolic freedom that did not have a daily-life counterpart (as in nude theatre), and by taking a financial profit from mass-produced imitation hip culture. "This is the 'liberal' version of Hitler's 'final solution' of the youth problem. . . . I say it is time for us to create our own culture, our own lives."

Dropping Out

On the whole, however, the counter culture proposed not so much a confrontation with mainstream culture as a simple withdrawal from it. As [social observer] Lawrence Lipton put it in 1968, "The hippies have passed beyond American society. They're not really living in the same society. . . . It's not so much that they're living on the leftovers, on the waste of American society, as that they just don't give a damn." Or, as [hippie author] Raymond Mungo wrote, "we . . . long ago commenced on our own total Moratorium on constructive participation in this society."

Withdrawal often meant heading for a hip commune. The communes, so the theory went, were not aimed at cultural confrontation, but simply were a turning away to build a new society apart from the old. Down on the commune, a hipster wrote in 1969, "We are in Amerika, but we are no longer a part of it."

From what were the hippies so alienated? Why did they see an alternative, be it confrontive or simply escapist, as necessary? The widespread sense of the counterculture was that it was simply impossible to cope with the dominant American culture any longer. America was a treadmill, a swamp of mediocrity, and emotional pressure cooker; it had become a series of meaningless institutions that transcended persons and developed lives of their own. Moreover, America had become Amerika (the German spelling evoked the Nazis), an oppressor of dissenters. Worse, it was all boring. Widespread mental illness and compulsive violence showed that there was a deep-running malaise in the culture; the rational alternative, as the hippies saw it, was simply to drop out.

But even dropping out was hard to do. Hippie communes were not welcome in many neighborhoods. Rock festivals were banned at every turn. Nonviolent psychedelic chemists ended up in prison. Establishment culture—which was, after all, in the driver's seat—was not willing to tolerate the deviant behavior of the new alternative. As one hippie wrote,

"They sense a threat to their continued . . . dominance. And they are absolutely correct."

The Generation Gap

Age did not a hippie make or unmake (there were, after all, a few older hippies and lots of young straights), but it is abundantly clear that most counterculturists were relatively young (under thirty, as the catchphrase had it) and that there was great distrust among the hippies of persons very far beyond adolescence. Many writers on both sides of the chasm depicted a "generation gap" that constituted a major battle-line between youth and adults. Theodore Roszak helped promote the concept in *The Making of a Counter Culture*, depicting as critical formative agents [beat poet] Allen Ginsberg's 1950s poem *Howl*, which condemned the parental generation by identifying it with the evil [biblical king] Moloch, and *Mad* magazine, which steadily presented a fairly consistent cynicism about "adult" culture to a very large young audience. Within the counterculture, the generation gap was much discussed. The old was moribund; revolutionary cultural change was imminent. One polemicist, Jack G. Burgess, proclaimed,

[You are standing on a generation that] WILL NOT BE STOOD UPON!

You have declared illegal virtually every establishment, event, gathering, device, and instrument we consider important and worthwhile.

[But] YOU CANNOT STOP THE HANDS OF TIME AND YOU CANNOT STILL THE WINDS OF CHANGE!

YOU ARE DYING! Time is removing you from the face of this earth.

In a more analytical frame of mind, underground writer George D. Maloney in 1968 pictured society as broadly divided by age groups into three major generations: under thirty, thirty to forty-five, and over forty-five. The problem of the thirty-to-forty-five generation, he argued, was a simple one: its members were children of the Depression, were unable to shake their preoccupation with security when prosperity returned, and thus were never much concerned with human values. Maloney saw as hopeless the impasse between "young" and "parental" generations, and proclaimed, "'Tis indeed the stuff of which revolutions are made."

The hopelessness of the parental generation was a common theme in the underground, but occasionally a note of a brighter future sounded. Andrew Kopkind, writing in *Rolling Stone* about the 1969 Woodstock festival, saw a phoenix of new culture rising from the ashes of "adult" American life:

> What is not illusionary is the reality of a new culture of opposition. It grows out of the disintegration of the old forms,

Who Is Getting High?

Timothy Leary was America's self-appointed psychedelic guru whose media-savvy pronouncements such as "Turn on, tune in, and drop out," appeared on 1960s posters, buttons, bumperstickers, and magazine articles. In the following excerpt from his groundbreaking book The Politics of Ecstasy, *Leary lists groups of people who were prone to experiment with LSD.*

To understand the psychedelic controversy, it is necessary to study the sociology of psychedelic drugs. Who wants to get high? Who wants to smoke marijuana? To eat peyote? To ingest LSD? What people comprise this new drug menace?

The young

The racially and nationally alienated

The creative

Over 90 percent of the users of psychedelic plants and drugs fall into at least one of these three categories.

The Young Want to Turn On

Over 50 percent of the American population is under the age of twenty-five. Ominous, isn't it? From 50 to 70 percent of the usage of marijuana and LSD is by the high school and college age group. Around 70 percent of the arrests and imprisonments for possession of psychedelic substances fall on the shoulders of those under the age of thirty. The whiskey-drinking menopausal imprison the pot-smoking youth. Meditate on this situation.

the vinyl and aerosol institutions that carry all the inane and destructive values of privatism; competition, commercialism, profitability and elitism. . . .

It's not a "youth thing" now but a generational event; chronological age is only the current phase. . . .

Children of Privilege

The hippies were mainly children of privilege, and their outlook reflected their heritage. They glorified poverty and

---

The Racially and Nationally Alienated Like to Turn On
Negroes, Puerto Ricans, American Indians. The usage of the psychedelic plants marijuana and peyote in these noble minority groups of the American society is high. The whiskey-drinking, white middle class imprisons those with different cultural and religious preferences. Meditate on this situation.

The Creative Have to Turn On
It is conservative to estimate that over 70 percent of nonacademic creative artists have used psychedelic substances in their work.
    Painters. Poets. Musicians. Dancers. Actors. Directors. Beatlebrows. The whiskey-drinking middlebrows imprison the growing edge. Meditate on this situation.

The Criminal and Psychedelic Drugs
The stereotyped picture of the marijuana smoker is that of a criminal type. The statistics do not support this myth. Marijuana is used by groups which are socially alienated from middle-aged values—youth, Negroes, Indians, creative artists—but few criminals. Alcohol is the drug of the middle-aged white criminal. The larcenous and the violent. Safecrackers and Marines. The economics of heroin leads the addict to steal. Few professional criminals smoke pot. Few pot smokers are criminals (except for the offense of changing their consciousness).

Timothy Leary, *The Politics of Ecstasy.* Berkeley, CA: Ronin, 1998.

sometimes lived in it; they championed the rights of racial minorities and, to some extent, women. But the movement came from a prosperous, white, male-defined segment of society. Perhaps it was inevitable that those who would reject middle-class comforts had to come from comfortable backgrounds; the have-nots of society had no material luxuries to rebel against.

Black hippies were unusual. They did show up occasionally, and they were readily accepted by the white majority. Their numbers, however, were never large. Blacks interested in dissent from the prevailing culture tended to be more interested in racial-political than flower-child activities. It is noteworthy, though, that militant blacks, while critical of all who would not join the revolutionary struggle, regarded the hippies as allies, not enemies. In 1968, an editorial in the *Black Panther*, the most widely read militant black publication, defined the Black Panther Party's position in its usual mince-no-words style:

> Black brothers stop vamping on the hippies. They are not your enemy. Your enemy, right now, is the white racist pigs who support this corrupt system. . . . Your enemy is not the hippies.
> . . . WE HAVE NO QUARREL WITH THE HIPPIES. LEAVE THEM ALONE. Or the BLACK PANTHER PARTY will deal with you!

Certainly the counterculture was male-defined. As the following chapters will suggest, authorship in the underground press was overwhelmingly male. Women were commonly "chicks"; when they were in relationships with men, they were "old ladies." It is important to remember, however, that the heyday of the counterculture, which was in the late 1960s, came along before the prominent advent of the contemporary feminist movement, which began to attract serious, widespread attention only about 1968 or 1969, just as the counterculture was starting to wind down. At least at first, the male hippies were as disinclined as males elsewhere in society to allow women equal rights and privileges; the gap between egalitarian hippie rhetoric and male hippie actions may have had some influence on the emerging feminists, many of whom had deep roots in the counterculture. If the writers quoted in subsequent chapters tend to be male, and if hippie ideas seem largely male-defined, it is because that was the dominant orientation of the hippies in their prime years. . . .

Dope and Drugs

Nothing else was so characteristic of the counterculture as dope. The overwhelming majority of hippies used it, and the few who didn't approved of its use by others. The commitment to—as opposed to furtive use of—dope was the single largest symbol of the difference between counterculture and Establishment culture.

The use of the term *dope* here instead of *drugs* is deliberate. To the hippies, it served to draw a line between the drugs perceived to be good and those deemed bad. Dope was good; drugs, on the other hand, included both good and bad substances. The distinction was imprecise, of course; hippies disagreed a great deal about where the line between good and bad should be drawn. Very generally, most hippies approved of such substances as marijuana, hashish, LSD, psilocybin, mescaline, peyote, and morning glory seeds; they were less approving, and often outspokenly critical, of amphetamines, methadrine, DMT, STP, barbiturates, the opiates, and sometimes cocaine. Psychedelics were good; speed and downers were bad. Substances that were perceived as expanding consciousness were good; things that made the user dumb were bad. But each individual made his or her own choices. There was no universally accepted dividing line between the two categories.

Tom Coffin was one hip writer who delineated the distinction between dope and drugs:

> We're talking about and doing Revolution, attack on all fronts, political, educational, religious, cultural, even *business*. . . . And dope is part of that revolution, and if you fear dope (Dope, not DRUGS—alcohol is a drug, pot is DOPE; nicotine is a DRUG, acid is DOPE; DRUGS turn you off, dull your senses, give you the strength to face another day in Death America, DOPE turns you on, heightens sensory awareness, sometimes twists them out of shape and you experience that too, gives you vision and

clarity, necessary to create Life from Death) if you fear DOPE more than you fear Richard Nixon and his Machined Men of Death, then you have indeed sold out and bought in. . . . The difference between Stupor and Ecstasy is the difference between Jack Daniels and Orange Sunshine [LSD], between the Pentagon and Woodstock, between *The New York Times* and *Good Times*. We all have to make our choices. . . .

Virtually everyone in the counterculture agreed that dope, whatever its correct name, was great. One all-star symposium sponsored by LEMAR International (the marijuana-legalization lobby), whose participants included Timothy Leary, Allen Ginsberg, Leslie Fiedler, Abbie Hoffman, and Jerry Rubin, "agreed that the biggest problem with drugs is shitty drug laws and the bad research." The counterculture saw the main "drug problems" as spotty quality and high prices.

Dope was utterly intrinsic to the counterculture. The hippies believed that dope itself had altered the consciousness of millions of individuals in fundamental ways, and that that alteration was inevitably a major force in the establishment of the new culture. So contended [LSD guru] Richard Alpert (later Ram Dass) when he wrote, "We've moved in the direction of a whole new model of the human brain. . . . You can travel anywhere, back into childhood, back through evolutionary history, cosmic history, down your own bloodstream or nervous system." And it made the new culture sweet. As [hip author] Jan Hodenfield wrote about the Woodstock festival, "Equal to the outside's anger and concern about the 'drug menace' was its awe at the 'politeness,' the 'good behavior,' the 'cheerfulness,' the 'lack of violence.' And the two were never connected."

Dope, though good, was never seen as problem-free. What was important was that the downside was dwarfed by the upside. As Raymond Mungo wrote, ". . . for us, everything is possible; if the heart is willing, what ecstatic adventure is too risky? *What is risk?*"

So dope was a constitutive element of the counterculture. As Leary put it, "You have to learn the outside dope which is TV, and the inside dope which are drugs, and if you don't someone's going to do it for you and they're going to cop [steal] your mind completely. That's why your only hope is dope."

From the perspective of a quarter-century later, it is easy to observe that the hippies were overly optimistic about the power dope held for good and naive about the downside of drugs in general. However, the hippies enunciated an ethic of drugs that made more overall sense than any ethics or policies prevailing in the drug-hysterical 1990s. The main elements of the hip ethics of dope looked something like this: Use it positively. Use it sanely. Know what you're doing. Avoid bad drugs. Avoid misuse of (good) dope. Don't use dope to hurt others. Assert your freedom to make your own decisions about dope. And have a good trip.

A Way of Life

A UCLA professor was quoted in the days of hip as saying that "if a young man hasn't smoked pot by the time he's twenty, he's probably sick," that is, "seriously neurotic," because marijuana is "a way of life for America's youth." Evidence from the hip era suggests that indeed huge numbers of the young were smoking it. A sample of 219 University of Kansas students in 1971 indicated that 69 percent had smoked marijuana and that 92 percent had friends who smoked it. A 1971 Gallup Poll reportedly found that over 40 percent of college students had tried pot, a percentage "eight times as high as [that] recorded in a 1967 survey." The College Poll found that in 1972, 60 percent of college students had used marijuana and noted that "the results of this annual drug study belie the theory that drug use on the campus is abating. It was generally thought that the drug culture was a unique one which would generally lose favor as the troubled era of the late 60s and early 1970s passed away. This now appears to be false."

The National Commission on Marijuana and Drug Abuse, in its extensive survey published in 1972, found that twenty-four million Americans had smoked marijuana; the incidence of use reached 40 percent in the eighteen-to-twenty-one age group, and 38 percent in the twenty-two-to-twenty-five age group. Lewis Yablonsky, in a study that specifically focused on the counterculture in 1968, found that 90.7 percent of his sample had used marijuana and that 68.2 percent had used LSD. All in all, dope achieved widespread use among youth in general and it was the common denominator of the counterculture.

Massive increases in arrests and border seizures accompanied the spread of dope. But neither stemmed the tide of dope. The New York *Times* estimated that 99 percent of the crowd at Woodstock were smoking marijuana, and a state police sergeant was quoted as commenting, "As far as I know, the narcotics guys are not arresting anybody for grass. If we did, there wouldn't be enough space in Sullivan County, or the next three counties, to put them in." Many hippies believed that they were looking the future directly in the eye: "The drug revolution is with us, despite border shutdowns, surveillance techniques, police, everything. It's a revolution that's sweeping the world."

Even before Woodstock, as early as 1967, hundreds could gather for smoke-ins without fear of arrest. Marijuana's sweet smoke permeated society; even Kim Agnew, the daughter of the staunchly antidope vice-president Spiro Agnew, was busted in 1969. . . .

The psychoactive properties of marijuana had been known in the United States since the turn of the century, but the use of grass had spread only very slowly until the 1960s. LSD and its unusual effects were discovered in 1938, but the chemical was hardly used until the middle 1960s, at which time it was still being sold legally. With the emergence of the counterculture, however, marijuana quickly spread to the point that hippies could boast that it was "so widely used, it's unofficially legal." And LSD wasn't far behind.

Chapter 3

Changing Lives

The Growth of the Women's Liberation Movement

Sara M. Evans

In the 1960s, millions of women fought to gain equal rights for African Americans, but women continued to encounter gender discrimination at home, at school, and on the job. Even in the revolutionary antiwar movement women were expected to cook, clean, take care of children, make coffee, and perform secretarial work. By the early 1970s, however, a growing number of feminists began to agitate for women's liberation. As Sara M. Evans, professor of history and director of the Center for Advanced Feminist Studies at the University of Minnesota writes, women were surprisingly successful in gaining legal protections in the early years of the movement.

By 1970 "women's lib" was on everyone's lips. Between January and March substantial stories on the women's liberation movement appeared in virtually every major journal and broadcast network. People were fascinated, intrigued, and often angered by the flamboyant tactics of feminist radicals. The combined effects of the women's liberation movement's agitation and the legal and legislative strategies of organizations such as the National Organization for Women [NOW] and the Women's Equity Action League [WEAL] appeared to be changing the landscape. In January a front-page article in the *New York Times* noted, "The walls of economic and psychological discrimination against women in the American job market are beginning to crack under the pressures of the Federal Government, the women's liberation movement, and the efforts of thousands of individual women themselves." The same day the article appeared, WEAL filed a complaint with the U.S. Department of Labor demanding a review of all colleges and universities holding federal contracts to determine whether they complied with antidiscrimination regulations. Two hundred and fifty institutions were targets for more specific charges of sex discrimination. By the end of the year, suits brought by women now willing to make public charges against discriminatory employers both for themselves individually and for women as a class had more than three hundred and sixty institutions of higher education in court.

While lawyers took to the courts, radical feminists grabbed headlines with more direct tactics: They had already "hexed" Wall Street and bridal fairs, disrupted congressional hearings to demand legalized abortion, conducted a rape speak-out where victims for the first time publicly shared their experiences, and announced self-defense karate classes for women. On March 18, 1970, two hundred women occupied the offices of the *Ladies' Home Journal* and stayed for eleven hours of sharp debate and negotiation. A journal for women, they argued, should provide day care for its own employees, pay a minimum of $125 a week, hire more minorities, and replace its male editor with an entirely female senior staff. As a result the *Journal* agreed to give them an eight-page supplement to the August 1970 issue. The editor, John Mack Carter, introduced the supplement with his own account of the encounter. "Beneath the shrill accusations and the radical dialectic, our editors heard some convincing truths about the persistence of sexual discrimination in many areas of American life." More important, perhaps, "we seemed to catch a rising note of angry self-expression among today's American women, a desire for representation, for recognition, for a broadening range of alternatives." The accompanying articles, written collectively, explored sex discrimination in the labor force and education, childbirth, divorce, appearance and beauty, love, sex, and how to start a consciousness-raising group.

With perfect timing the *Journal* special issue coincided with the fiftieth anniversary of the passage of the Nineteenth

Amendment to the Constitution granting women the right to vote. When the National Organization for Women called for a Women's Strike for Equality on August 26, 1970, the new movement suddenly gained visibility, setting off another round of explosive growth. Thousands of women marched and demonstrated in cities across the country, some of them taking a stand for the first time in their lives; others, former suffragists, had waited a long time to march again for women's rights. Following the strike, new members flooded into NOW chapters bringing into the organization members of the younger generation who had shaped the radical branch of women's liberation.

It Was Contagious

Women's liberation was contagious. When a *Newsweek* writer began to work on a story on the movement she discovered that many of her colleagues were preparing an EEOC [Equal Employment Opportunity Commission] complaint against *Newsweek*. With careful planning they held a press conference to announce their complaint just as *Newsweek* hit the stands with a major story on women's liberation. [Reporter] Sophy Burnham laughed when she received an assignment from *Redbook* to do a story on the women's movement. "A lunatic fringe," she thought. But "within a week I was so upset, I could hardly focus my ideas." In four months of listening to women's anger, pain, and quest for identity "chords were struck that I had thought long dead. . . . I thought I had come to terms with my life; but every relationship—husband, child, father, mother—was brought into question." By the end she was a convert: "I am now offended by things that would never have bothered me before. I am now a feminist. I am infused with pride—in my sisters, in myself, in my womanhood."

The power of the women's movement lay in its capacity to stimulate such deep rethinking, to pose, *as a problem*, concepts such as femininity and motherhood and relationships previously taken for granted. Most Americans, both male and female, unlike Sophy Burnham, were not converted. They were angry, defensive, confused, but they were thinking about gender nonetheless. Millions tuned in on September 20, 1973, to watch tennis star Billie Jean King battle Bobby Riggs, a 1939 Wimbledon winner and defender of manhood. Riggs had brilliantly hustled the media with his taunts against King's campaign for more opportunities and more money for women tennis professionals. "You insist that top women players provide a brand of tennis comparable to men's. I challenge you to prove it. I contend that you not only cannot beat a top male player, but that you can't beat me, a tired old man." Though the odds in Las Vegas were 5 to 2 for Riggs; King won three sets with ease, 6–4, 6–3, 6–3. Riggs' rout in this "battle of the sexes" sparked debates, and female pride, in households and workplaces across the country.

Raising Consciousness

The central organizing tool of the women's liberation movement, the small consciousness-raising group, proved an effective mechanism for movement building. Within such groups, women discovered that their experiences were not unique but part of a larger pattern, and they rediscovered female community. The intensity and power of the new bonds among women prompted them to name themselves a sisterhood, a familial metaphor for an emerging social and political identity that captured the key qualities of egalitarianism, love, and mutual responsibility. Because the groups had little or no structure, they could be formed anywhere—from offices to churches to neighborhoods. In effect, consciousness-raising defined the personal issues of daily life—housework, child rearing, sexuality, etiquette, even language—as political issues susceptible to collective action and solution. Nothing was beyond discussion.

This spreading debate in thousands of formal and informal small groups soon affected informal female networks such as office friendships, religious groups, neighborhood kaffeeklatsches, and other voluntary associations. The new feminism necessitated extensive redefinition of roles, attitudes, and values because the traditional definitions of women and men were so at odds with women's actual experience. Women, in effect, reintroduced the personal experience of being female into the political discourse of the day, challenging the obsolete language that [divided] public and private life along lines of gender. Their debates brought new analyses to the questions raised by earlier feminisms. Among themselves, feminists argued vehemently about whether the division between public and private was universal or particular to American society in recent times, and whether women were essentially different from or the same as men. The heat of their debate opened new windows on women's lives as individuals and as citizens and marked the difficulty of devising new categories for their changing reality.

Political Momentum

The new feminist movement continued to gain momentum in the early part of the 1970s. There were more rallies and demonstrations in behalf of women's rights every year until they peaked in 1975 with more than three hundred nationally reported feminist events. Legislative victories, however, probably reached an apex in 1972. After decades of inattention, Congress suddenly recognized the political power of women and the importance of women's claims for equity. The feminist political awakening frightened lawmakers who rushed to appease a constituency that potentially represented more than half of the voting public, making it possible to gain hearings, votes, and legislative victories with breathtaking speed. While the media explained and explored the meaning of consciousness-raising and arguments over the use of "Ms." instead of "Miss" and "Mrs.," Congress passed more legislation in behalf of women's rights than it had considered seriously for decades. The ranks of ERA [Equal Rights Amendment to the Constitution] supporters now included the League of Women Voters, Business and Professional Women, the YWCA, the American Association of University Women, Common Cause, and the United Auto Workers, a coalition capable of mounting a massive two-year campaign that generated more mail on Capitol Hill than the Vietnam war. On March 22, 1972, Congress finally approved the ERA. By the end of the year, twenty-two of the needed thirty-five states had ratified it.

Other women's rights legislation passed by Congress in 1972 included Title IX of the Higher Education Act, providing "No person in the United States shall, on the basis of sex, be excluded from participation in, be denied the benefits of, or be subjected to discrimination under any education program or activity receiving federal financial assistance," setting the stage for the growth of women's athletics later in the decade. An Equal Opportunity Act broadened the jurisdiction of the EEOC and strengthened its enforcement capacity. And working parents received a tax break for their child-care expenses. Representative Bella Abzug recalled 1972 as "a watershed year. We put sex discrimination provisions into everything. There was no opposition. Who'd be against equal rights for women? So we just kept passing women's rights legislation."

Abzug, a flamboyant activist who had belonged to [the antiwar group] Women Strike for Peace in the 1960s, joined with [NOW founder] Betty Friedan and Representative Shirley Chisholm in 1971 to found the National Women's Political Caucus (NWPC). A bipartisan organization intended to increase female visibility and participation in the political arena, the NWPC further demonstrated women's political strength in 1972: The proportions of women attending the national party conventions that summer jumped to 40 percent in the Democratic party (up from 13 percent in 1968) and 30 percent in the Republican party (up from 17 percent in 1968). That year Representative Shirley Chisholm mounted the first serious presidential campaign by a black woman. Texas state legislator Sissy Farenthold, a surprise nomination for vice president from the floor of the Democratic Convention, received 420 delegate votes. And both political parties, which had virtually ignored women four years before, adopted most of the NWPC platform including planks for ratification of the ERA, antidiscrimination legislation, elimination of tax inequities, educational equity for women, and extension of the Equal Pay Act. They balked only on the issue of abortion.

When the Supreme Court handed down its decision [legalizing] abortion in *Roe v. Wade* in 1973, it seemed that fem-

A Busy Year for Women's Rights

Nineteen seventy-two was an important year for supporters of women's equality. Congress passed several bills that prohibited discrimination against women in education and the workplace. Women also began to make strides in reproductive freedom, religious expression, and politics. The following excerpt lists some of the major achievements accomplished by the women's liberation movement in 1972.

- Congress passes the Equal Rights Amendment, first introduced in 1923; Hawaii is the first state to ratify.
- The Equal Employment Opportunity Act of 1972 empowers the EEOC to go to court with discrimination cases.
- Title IX of the Education Amendments of 1972 is passed, prohibiting sex discrimination in most federally assisted educational programs. Opens up a debate in the area of sports that remains unresolved throughout the decade. . . .
- The Equal Pay Act of 1963 is extended to cover administrative, professional and executive employees. . . .
- *Ms.* magazine publishes its Preview Issue.
- The University of Minnesota lets women into the marching band.
- The Maritime College of the State University of New York admits women.
- Women's Lobby, Inc., is formed by Carol Burris to lobby Congress on women's issues.
- The Civil Rights Commission is given jurisdiction over sex discrimination. Loses jurisdiction over abortion in 1978.
- Women's issues, including the right to abortion, are included in the platform of *La Raza Unida*, a Mexican-American political movement, as the result of pressure from its Chicana caucus.
- Sally Priesand is first woman ordained a rabbi.
- Marlo Thomas and friends produce the record "Free to Be . . . You and Me," the first record of nonsexist, multiracial songs, poems, and stories for children.
- The *Washington Post* eliminates sex-segregated classified ads.

- New York City is the scene of the First International Festival of Women's Films.
- Shirley Chisholm runs for President.
- Women are 40 percent of the delegates to the Democratic National Convention (13 percent in 1968); 35 percent of the Republican.
- Frances ("Sissy") Farenthold comes in second in Democratic Convention Vice-Presidential nomination.
- Jean Westwood is unanimously selected chair of Democratic National Committee (first woman in either party).
- Margo St. James and other prostitutes start COYOTE (Cut Out Your Old Tired Ethics).
- Judy Chicago, Miriam Schapiro, and members of the Feminist Art Program at the California Institute of the Arts open 17-room *Womanhouse* exhibit seen by 4,000. . . .
- American Heritage publishes first dictionary (a wordbook for children) to define "sexism," include the phrase "liberated women," and recognize "Ms."
- Ms. Foundation is formed, only nationwide funding source specifically for women.
- League of Women Voters endorses the ERA.
- Gail and Thomas Parker are appointed president and vice-president respectively of Bennington College (Vermont)—first wife-husband team.
- Revised Order 4 requires companies doing business with the federal government to form written affirmative action programs for hiring and promoting minorities and women.
- First conference of Older Women's Liberation held in New York City. . . .
- Women elected to Congress are Elizabeth Holtzman (D.-N.Y.), Yvonne Brathwaite Burke (D.-Calif.), Barbara Jordan (D.-Tex.), Patricia Schroeder (D.-Col.), and Marjorie Holt (R.-Md.).
- On the tenth anniversary of her suicide, Marilyn Monroe becomes the subject of articles, poems, and books analyzing her victimization as a sex symbol.

Suzanne Levine and Harriet Lyons, eds., *The Decade of Women*. New York: G.P. Putnam's Sons, 1980.

inists had a golden touch. Jane Roe, a pseudonym for a pregnant, single woman in Dallas County, Texas, had brought a federal suit claiming that the Texas criminal abortion laws unconstitutionally abridged her personal privacy by denying her the right to a medically safe abortion. She sued "on behalf of herself and all other women" in the same situation. The *New York Times* editorialized that "the Court's seven-to-two ruling [invalidating state laws that prohibit abortion in the first three months of pregnancy] could bring to an end the emotional and divisive public argument over what always should have been an intensely private and personal matter." Though the Court's ruling followed a rather dramatic shift in public opinion, however, it propelled into action a deeply convinced minority opposed to abortion. The boundary separating issues that should be subjects of public policy and state control from those that properly remained private concerns continued to be a contested one.

Division over women's changing roles, in fact, was just beginning, not about to end. Its terms, however, were new. Joseph Adelson, writing a hostile article in the *New York Times Magazine* entitled "Is Women's Lib a Passing Fad?", dismissed some feminist goals as "banal simply because everyone seems to agree with them, men and women and alike.... Everyone believes in equal pay for equal work; most everyone believes that women should not be sharply limited in the economic roles available to them; and so on." Such words delighted and frustrated feminists who knew that these issues were hardly "banal" and that they did not represent the reality for most women. Adelson went on to argue against feminist advocates of "radical changes in sexual socialization and identity [and] radical changes in the family."

These more disruptive ideas were being discussed and experimented with primarily among feminists who chose to work outside the legislative halls and political parties. Like feminists in the 1910s, these younger women were bent on challenging the system of gender in its broadest dimensions, and they saw specific legislative reforms as too limited and short-term. Theirs was a cultural radicalism. They wanted to transform the very definition of "female" and to shatter every barrier to women's autonomy—not just laws, but attitudes and values, methods of child rearing, marriage, and sexual norms. They operated in an atmosphere of radical experimentalism critical of virtually all existing institutions and determined to reclaim female power and liberate women's erotic potential. The meaning of female autonomy and authentic femininity varied dramatically according to whether they assumed that women were fundamentally the same or fundamentally different from men. Debates raged, groups split and reformed around different ideological constellations. Some, especially those most committed to continued alliance with other groups in the anti-Vietnam War movement and the student new left, joined more moderate feminist reformers in a deep suspicion of any assertion of female difference, knowing how it had historically been used . . . to assert female inferiority. Yet others chose to use the process of consciousness-raising to comprehend and give political meaning to their own experiences. All of these efforts, however, by emphasizing "women" as a group, and implicitly assuming a white and middle-class norm, obscured differences *among* women along lines of race, class, and ethnicity.

Forming a Community of Women

The power of female solidarity and community in consciousness-raising groups, and such groups' insistence on examining the world from women's point of view, led to an emphasis on issues uniquely female. Rape, wrote Susan Griffin in 1970, "is a kind of terrorism which severely limits the freedom of women and makes women dependent on men." Such issues required female-controlled environments such as rape crisis centers and shelters for battered women within which women could be empowered to resist oppression and work for change. Like women reformers in the nineteenth century, feminists created institutions in response to women's unmet needs and their desire to be free from dependence on male-dominated institutions and ideas.

Thus outside the framework of traditional electoral politics, feminists began to construct a new public terrain giving priority to issues affecting women's lives and issues previously kept outside public surveillance. Rape crisis centers, battered women's shelters, women's health clinics, and feminist publications, coffee houses, and bookstores suddenly appeared in cities across the country. In Boston a women's health collective wrote a book to help women make knowledgeable decisions about their own bodies and health care alternatives. After selling two hundred thousand copies in a newsprint edition from a nonprofit press, *Our Bodies, Ourselves* came out in a commercial, revised edition in 1973. Its fourth edition was published in 1984. Another health collective formed in Chicago to advise women seeking abortions—before *Roe v. Wade* made them legal—soon began to provide the abortions themselves. Acting on their own behalf and in their own space, women discovered that their space was very wide indeed.

The emphasis on the personal nature of political action, reminiscent of the civil rights movement, empowered lesbians to pursue the sexual revolution begun in the sixties and proclaim the political importance of sexual preference. Although lesbians battled continually in the more formally structured, moderate wing of feminism for visibility and recognition of their oppression, in the radical branch of the movement, their struggle led to separatism. Those, like Charlotte Bunch, who "came out" and proclaimed their lesbianism after joining the women's liberation movement, "did not realize how savagely we would be disinherited by our 'sisters'." Lesbian feminists argued that lesbianism represented the most complete form of female autonomy. They called attention to the exploitation of homophobia as a means of undermining feminism. . . . The charge that women who challenge traditional gender boundaries were lesbians (and that lesbians were somehow "unnatural") had been used to contain feminist insurgency throughout the twentieth century. "As long as the label 'dyke' can be used to frighten women into a less militant stand, keep her separate from her sisters, keep her from giving primacy to anything other than men and family—then to that extent she is controlled by the male culture."

Lesbian collectives such as the Furies in Washington,

D.C., recognized that lesbians themselves had to struggle for a new identity against the grain of cultural prejudice and began an exploration of the meaning of lesbian community, identity, and sexuality. "As separatists, we stopped trying to justify our lives to straight society and instead concentrated on ourselves." Together they could move beyond the haunting fears of discovery and rejection, the self-hatred and invisibility inflicted by a culture that labeled them abnormal. Together they could claim, celebrate, and explore the meaning of their sexuality that the rest of society seemed to find so frightening. As they announced and defended their love for other women, they also explored barriers to female autonomy and female community restricting heterosexual women as well. Soon lesbian feminism informed the central theoretical debates within the movement.

Birth of the Environmental Movement

Philip Shabecoff

The booming material prosperity of the United States in the 1950s and 1960s left a legacy of severe industrial pollution that was largely ignored by the government. Skies over major cities were dark with smog, oceans bubbled brown with industrial sludge, and the Cuyahoga River in Cleveland, Ohio, was so full of chemicals that it actually burst into flames. It seemed as if a new threat to the environment made headlines nearly every day. When the turbulent sixties came to an end, scores of baby boomers—a number of whom protested against the war—now had children of their own. As scores of social activists turned their attention to cleaning up the polluted environment, millions of Americans were educated to the necessities of clean air and water. Within a few short years, city, state, and federal agencies began to monitor and regulate air and water pollution.

In the excerpt below, Philip Shabecoff, environmental reporter for the *New York Times* and executive publisher of *Greenwire*, a daily environmental news service, explores the founding of the environmental movement and the legislative successes that followed.

On April 22, 1970, a crisp, sunny day over much of the country, some 20 million Americans, many of them young, massed in the streets, on campuses, on riverbanks, in parks, and in front of government and corporate buildings to demonstrate their distress and anxiety over the state of the environment. It was called Earth Day. A revolution, of sorts, had begun.

From "Saving Ourselves," in *A Fierce Green Fire: The American Environmentalist Movement*, by Philip Shabecoff. Copyright © 1993 by Philip Shabecoff. Reprinted by permission of Hill and Wang, a division of Farrar, Straus and Giroux, LLC.

Earth Day was not a spontaneous uprising. The sense of mounting ecological crisis had begun to penetrate the national consciousness well before. [There was] growing concern and activity [by] environmental groups and the government in the 1960s. A series of well-publicized ecological insults in the years following publication of [Rachel Carson's groundbreaking book on harmful pesticides in the environment] *Silent Spring*—including a huge spill from an oil rig off the coast of Santa Barbara, California, the Cuyahoga River in Cleveland bursting into flames because of the heavy concentration of inflammable industrial chemicals in its waters, the choking of Lake Erie by phosphates, the dumping of toxic PCBs into the Hudson and Housatonic rivers, the dense smog blanketing many of our major cities, the contamination of food fish by mercury, the fouling of beaches by sewage, and dozens of other notorious episodes—directed the country's attention to the worsening condition of the natural landscape.

The conservation movement was a response to nineteenth-century abuses of the land and its resources. The twentieth century would turn out to be far more dangerous to the natural environment and to the humans and other creatures that live within it. A few names and phrases evoke the environmental havoc wrought during this century: Killer smog. The Dust Bowl. The Cuyahoga River. Bhopal. Toxic waste. Three Mile Island. Chernobyl. PCBs. Love Canal. Times Beach. The *Exxon Valdez*. Lead paint. DDT. Minimata disease. Radioactive waste. Whales and dolphins. Gridlock. Rain forests. Inner city. Acid rain. Asbestos. Garbage mountains. Endangered species. Mass extinction. Strip mines. The ozone layer. The greenhouse effect. The possibility of a "nuclear winter." Threats to the environment sped far ahead of their solutions, overmatching the strength of the fledgling conservation movement.

Individual citizens were already expressing alarm and anger over the insults done to the natural world by human mistakes, excesses and abuses of technology, and the economy.

Smog and other pollution were suffocating a growing number of cities and producing pressures for action on political leaders. . . .

Even President Nixon, no tree hugger, found it expedient to declare in his February 1970 State of the Union message that the 1970s "absolutely must be the years when America pays its debt to the past by reclaiming the purity of its air, its waters and our living environment. It is literally now or never." His cabinet secretary, John C. Whitaker, later recalled, "When President Nixon and his staff walked into the White House on January 20, 1969, we were totally unprepared for the tidal wave of public opinion in favor of cleaning up the environment that was about to engulf us."

"Do We Want to Live or Die?"

But April 22, 1970, is as good a date as any to point to as the day environmentalism in the United States began to emerge as a mass social movement. The American people, demonstrating the power of a democracy to address a social crisis, started taking matters into their own hands. The time had come to save ourselves.

Much later, Earth Day would be described by Denis Hayes, the national coordinator of the event, as "the largest organized demonstration in human history." It may or may not have been the largest such event in history, but "organized" is hardly the word for the varied and often highly inventive happenings staged by demonstrators around the country to express their distress over ecological threats. The day was chiefly and surprisingly lighthearted. Participants picked up litter, planted trees, and adorned themselves with flowers. In San Francisco, a group calling itself the "Environmental Vigilantes" poured oil into a reflecting pool in front of the offices of the Standard Oil Company of California to protest the oil slicks discoloring offshore waters. In Tacoma, Washington, a hundred high school students rode horses down a superhighway to call attention to pollution from automobiles. Junior high school students in White Plains, New York, painted a ramshackle railroad station and cleaned up the trash surrounding it.

Many of the day's activities focused on the dangers of pollution to human health, the issue that would be at the core of the new broad-based environmentalism. On Fifth Avenue in New York City, demonstrators held up dead fishes to symbolize the contamination of the Hudson River and shouted to passersby, "You're next, people!" New York's Mayor John Lindsay gave a speech in which he stated that "beyond words like ecology, environment and pollution there is a simple question: do we want to live or die?"

With Earth Day, the fears and frustrations felt by the American people after years of environmental neglect began to shape a new political energy. After Earth Day, nothing was the same. The demonstrations of that April day forced government and industry to open the gates of change, however slowly and grudgingly. The millions of Earth Day demonstrators touched off a great burst of activism that profoundly affected the nation's laws, its economy, its corporations, its farms, its politics, science, education, religion, and journalism, created new institutions, and, in time, changed the physical world itself by reducing pollution and preserving open space and other resources. Most important, the social forces unleashed after Earth Day changed, probably forever, the way Americans think about the environment. We now look at a safe and aesthetically pleasing environment not only as necessary to our happiness and well-being but as a right due us along with freedom and opportunity.

In the years following Earth Day, environmentalism, once regarded as the self-serving indulgence of a privileged elite, became "America's cause," . . . an expanding mass movement that could in the not too distant future become one of the dominant features of the nation's political life. Although environmentalism certainly was born long before April 22, 1970, it takes no great license to proclaim that day the dawn of the environmental era. . . .

A Sense of Social Justice

Denis Hayes believes that the energy that exploded on Earth Day sprang from the social activism on the nation's campuses and the restless discontent of the young.

> There was this broad, sort of all-encompassing sense that things were falling apart. We got a charge of new life in the Kennedy era as we were all getting out of high school and

then there was this whole string of assassinations, finding ourselves up to our gills in a land war in Asia, seeing the racial situation in this country becoming increasingly polarized and watching—I don't know—just the general deterioration of the quality of life . . . somehow, this concern with the environment and the quality, as opposed to the mere quantity, of what was being produced by society seemed to capture that.

Many of the young activists who leaped into the crusade to save the environment shortly before or immediately after Earth Day and who now provide much of the leadership of the national environmental groups did so out of a broad sense of social justice rather than a specific interest in pollution and resource issues. Richard Ayres, a founder of the Natural Resources Defense Council and one of the many Yale University Law School graduates to become a professional environmentalist, explained that in the 1960s "there was a whole series of issues which people my age saw as part of one seamless web of need for social change—ending the war, a better criminal justice system, dealing with poverty and protecting the environment, which was a newly emerging or reemerging issue at the time." Ayres, a boyish-looking and deceptively mild-mannered crusader, and David Hawkins, another lawyer who joined the Natural Resources Defense Council in the early months of its existence, spent virtually all of the 1970s and 1980s at the center of the political and legal struggle to strengthen the Clean Air Act and to make it work effectively.

The links between the Earth Day activists and the other causes of the 1960s, including the antiwar, civil rights, Native American rights, and feminist movements, were direct. Pollution and the exploitation of public resources to create private wealth were regarded as expressions of social inequity. James Gustave (Gus) Speth, another founder of the Natural Resources Defense Council and later chairman of the Council on Environmental Quality and then president of a think tank called the World Resources Institute, recalled that the idea of an organization devoted to litigating for a safer, cleaner environment came to him one day in the late 1960s while reading an article in *The New York Times* about the NAACP [National Association for Advancement of Colored People] Legal Defense Fund. A few pages later there was a story about the environment and, said Speth, "it just occurred to me that there really should be an NAACP Legal Defense Fund for the environment."

To Speth, "unregulated discharge pipes, fish kills, urban air pollution, all kinds of industrial pollution—those were the issues that originally turned my head. It was not establishing wilderness areas in Montana." Yet like many militant new environmentalists, he was also appalled by the aesthetic degradation of the landscape. He had grown up in rural South Carolina before going to Yale, and "coming out of this beautiful pristine area and hitting the Northeast megalopo-

In the 1970s, demonstrators protested the polluting of water and air and advocated legislative measures to protect the environment.

lis up there in New Haven and looking at all the pollution in Bridgeport . . . I remember it shocked me.". . .

A Cause for Baby Boomers

The environmental impulse that came to a boil on Earth Day, however, has many roots other than the social unrest and campus revolts of the 1960s. Samuel Hays has pointed out that new values arose among the increasingly affluent Americans of the post–World War II period, many with greater leisure and higher levels of education than the pre-war norm, who demanded different consumer "amenities" than industry was providing. These included improved standards of health and physical fitness, better living conditions generally, and wider opportunities for recreation and leisure. While this was only one tendril of the flowering environmental movement, it was crucial because it helps explain why a great many Americans who were wary of joining other social causes of the period and tended to remain on the sidelines enthusiastically supported this one. Sociologist Denton E. Morrison commented that the environmental crusade "came as something of a relief to a movement-pummeled white, middle-class America and its representatives in the power structure. The environmental movement especially seemed to have potential for diverting the energies of a substantial portion of young people away from more bothersome movements and into [groups] that seemed to stand for something close to Country, God, Motherhood, and Apple Pie, and that, at worst, were still clearly the safest movement in town."

Many Americans responded to the rallying cry of Earth Day not because of any aesthetic or mystical affinity for nature, to fight for social justice, or to search for new consumer amenities or a more pleasant lifestyle, but out of fear—fear of cancer or other disease caused by toxic substances, fear for the future of their children, and fear that the value of their property would be diminished by pollution or inappropriate development. Americans who worried about [cancer-causing chemicals such as] PCBs in mother's milk, about polybrominated biphenyls [similar to PCBs] in Michigan cattle, about poisons leaking from rusty drums in their backyards, or about strontium 90 from atmospheric testing of nuclear weapons or radiation from Three Mile Island were not asking for new consumer items. They were expressing outrage and demanding change.

The older conservation groups—the Sierra Club, the National Audubon Society, the National Wildlife Federation, the Izaak Walton League, and others—played little or no role in Earth Day and, in fact, were surprised by the surge of national emotion. Still preoccupied by traditional land and wildlife preservation issues, most—although not all—of the old guard had remained blind and deaf to the growing national anger over pollution and other environmental threats to human health.

"We were taken aback by the speed or suddenness with which the new forces exploded," Michael McCloskey, then executive director and later chairman of the Sierra Club, recalled during an interview in 1989. The club had reemerged on the national scene in the 1960s, he recalled, by taking on and winning fights to preserve national parks and defend the beauty of the Grand Canyon. In the [mid-1960s] "the watchword became recreation and then natural beauty and environmental quality and all of that." Then, suddenly, there was a "whole new agenda" that seemed to have nothing to do with the old issues, an agenda that focused almost exclusively on pollution and waste, he said. "We were severely disoriented suddenly to find that all sorts of new personalities were emerging to lead something new, mainly people out of the youth rebellion of the 1960s who had all sorts of notions that just came out of nowhere . . . I remember being amazed at a meeting of a New Orleans group when someone said, 'Oh, we're not using paper napkins anymore. You can't do that.' I said, 'What's wrong with paper napkins?' 'Oh, that's the new ecology movement that says we can't do that.'"

For their part, the young militants who joined the movement during the Earth Day period tended to look at the old conservation groups as irrelevant. Denis Hayes, who would also organize the national celebration of the twentieth anniversary of Earth Day in 1990, recalled that "by and large, there was, I think, a pretty deep amount of ignorance of all of that and even some tendency to sort of distance themselves from the rest they termed 'the birds and squirrels people.'"

Saving Land, Preserving Nature

In remarkably few years, the fissure between the traditional conservation groups and the pollution- and public health-oriented activist national organizations was narrowed and largely—although not entirely—closed. Those concerned with public lands and wildlife realized that air and water pollution did not stop at the boundaries of the national parks and that Americans deprived of their health by industrial poisons could not enjoy the wonders of nature. The social militants, for their part, soon discovered that the assaults of technology and commerce on the environment were inevitably also attacks upon human beings; that oil spills that destroyed wildlife in Alaska and strip-mined mountains in Appalachia were part of the same abuse of the natural environment that threatened the health of people living in cities or workers in their factories. Just as [early environment crusaders] George Perkins Marsh, John Muir, Aldo Leopold, René Dubos, Rachel Carson, and others had foretold, human beings were not isolated from the natural world and the injuries they inflicted upon it. The cause of reducing pollution and protecting public health was clearly inseparable from the cause of saving the land and preserving nature. The principles of ecology, both scientific and moral, welded the old and the new environmentalism into a movement of fiercely competing but relatively unified national organizations.

The passions that swept through the nation's campuses in April 1970 soon died. Within a few months, young, middle-class Americans in and emerging from the universities once again grew increasingly self-absorbed and sought individual rewards rather than social reform. Especially during the Reagan era [in the 1980s], that search for individual fulfillment centered on the accumulation of wealth and material possessions. . . .

But the environmental movement, despite predictions that it would collapse, particularly during the energy crises of the 1970s, did not fade away. A chain reaction had started on Earth Day and, while it was slowed from time to time, it could not be broken by the apathy of the erstwhile student activists, the long lines at gasoline filling stations [in the late 1970s], the short attention span of a public conditioned by television, or even by the hostility and active opposition of a President of the United States. The interest and anger displayed by millions of Americans had caused the politicians, the news media, the universities, and other power centers to pay heed. With each passing year the environmental impulse become more deeply enmeshed in the nation's institutions, its laws, and its daily life.

In the aftermath of Earth Day, new environmental institutions such as Greenpeace emerged that combined a strong social sensibility with concern for the natural world. Political agendas that embraced the environment, such as social ecology, gained new adherents. The environmental movement itself soon began to grow a radical wing.

Religion, science, education, communications—virtually all sectors of American society found themselves changed by its power.

The Seventies Baby Bust

David Frum

The baby boomers were part of the largest population "bubble" in history. Many of them grew up in suburbs where women were expected to forego careers in order to have babies and raise families. But after the social revolution of the 1960s, fewer and fewer baby boomers were willing to emulate their parents and start families of their own. As David Frum, contributing editor at the *Weekly Standard* and senior fellow at the Manhattan Institute, writes in the following excerpt, this phenomenon led to a "baby bust" in the 1970s. This rapid decline in the birthrate is one reason some social critics called the seventies the "Me Decade," which implied baby boomers were self-centered and selfish.

Think of all those old movies in which a beautiful young wife looks up at her husband with dewy eyes and says, "Darling, I have some wonderful news." In the movies of the 1970s, pregnancy is not so happy. Actress after actress discovers that the child she is carrying is quite literally Satanic. In *Rosemary's Baby*, a pregnant Mia Farrow learns that the baby she's carrying is the Antichrist. In *The Omen*, Gregory Peck and Lee Remick make the same dreadful discovery about their child. Monster-babies drive the plot of the 1970s cult classic, *It's Alive!* And of course a demonic child was the star of one of the decade's most hugely successful movies, *The Exorcist*.

It's hard to remember an era when American popular culture was as nervous of children as in the 1970s. The protagonists of all the most successful situation comedies of the 1970s—*The Mary Tyler Moore Show*, *The Bob Newhart Show*,

From *How We Got Here: The Seventies, the Decade That Brought You Modern Life— for Better or Worse*, by David Frum. Copyright © 2000 by David Frum. Reprinted by permission of Basic Books, a member of Perseus Books, L.L.C., and Random House Canada, a division of Random House Canada Limited.

Rhoda, The Jeffersons, Three's Company—were cast as child-less. (The exceptions prove the rule: *All in the Family*'s Gloria announced her pregnancy in the show's 110th episode, in an attempt to perk up ratings. . . . With tens of millions of baby-boomer women entering their peak fertility years, statisticians expected a follow-on boomlet beginning in the middle 1970s. Instead, the number of twenty-something women rose and rose while the number of births dropped and dropped. Fewer babies were born in 1971 than in 1970, fewer in 1972 than in 1971, fewer in 1973 than in 1972. The number of births hit bottom in 1974, when just 3.1 million babies were born, down from 4.3 million in 1957. Eighteen New York City hospitals closed their maternity wards in the early 1970s. The total U.S. birth rate plunged to the lowest level seen since the 1930s, to *half* the level that prevailed in the 1950s.

People bear fewer children in economically troubled times. But the Americans of the 1970s did not merely postpone children, as the Americans of the 1930s did. They actually changed their minds about wanting them. In 1945, half of all adult Americans thought the ideal family contained four or more children. As late as 1967, 40 percent of Americans—and 45 percent of American women—thought that four or more was the ideal family. Six years later, in 1973, only 20 percent of American adults—and only 12 percent of college-educated women—thought that four or more children was the ideal. A majority of Americans thought two children ideal in 1980; back in 1936, only 29 percent would have been content for two. The Americans most immune to the economic woes of the 1970s actually turned against childbearing most strongly. In 1971, upper-crust Bryn Mawr conducted a survey of the college's five most recent graduating classes (1966, '67, '68, '69, and '70). About three-quarters of the alumnae participated. They reported giving birth to more than seventy babies. In 1975, the college repeated the survey of recent graduates (1971, '72, '73, '74, '75). Again, three-quarters of the alumnae responded. This time, they reported a grand total of *three* babies.

"Motherhood: Who Needs It?"

Abortion and birth control are obviously part of the explanation of the baby bust, but only a part. New York State liberalized its abortion law in 1970, and other states soon followed. The U.S. Supreme Court handed down *Roe v. Wade* in January 1973, which recognized abortion as a federal constitutional right. Abortion, once a crime so dreadful as to verge on the unmentionable, edged toward the center of sexual life. In 1975, federal statisticians counted 272 abortions for every one thousand live births; in 1976, they counted 312. New York City recorded 676 abortions for every one thousand births in 1976; in Washington, D.C., the number of abortions actually *equaled* the number of live births. From the late 1970s until the mid-1990s, the number of abortions in the United States seldom dipped below the 1.5 million mark.

Nevertheless, it would be a big mistake to seek a technological explanation for the crash in the birth rate. The women of the 1950s and early 1960s had big families not because they lacked the means to control their fertility—in that case, they would have borne nine or fourteen children apiece rather than three or four—but because they wanted big families. Married women had ready access to diaphragms, and even unmarried women could get them with only a little trouble. . . . The birth-control pill appeared on the market in 1961, a decade before the birth rate plunged.

It was women's preferences, not contraceptive techniques, that changed in the 1970s. The women of the 1970s wanted small families—often, they wanted no family at all. Only 50 percent of non-college young women and only 35 percent of college-educated young women regarded having children as "very important" in 1973. These women were unenthusiastic about children because they believed, perfectly correctly, that children would inhibit their freedom and compromise their individuality. "Motherhood: Who Needs It?" demanded Betty Rollins in a famous 1970 article in *Look*. "Even the most adorable children make for additional demands, complications, and hardships in the lives of even the most loving parents." Theologian Rosemary Radford Ruether, argued in her 1975 book *New Woman, New Earth*, "Each generation of women has been sacrificed to its own children. History has been the holocaust of women." It was past time, she and others felt, for the holocaust to end. The adults of the 1970s were adamant: Their needs came first. The truest single detail in a film packed with reminiscences of 1970s daily life, *The Ice Storm*, was the middle-class dinner party at which the children carried and cleared the plates for their parents' friends. In 1973, it would have seemed excruciatingly pretentious to hire a tuxedoed waiter to serve dinner in a private home and shockingly retrograde for the woman of the house to do it. The solution (almost unthinkable in the child-obsessive 1990s) was to assign the task to the kids.

"If a mother has a life of her own, the daughter will love her more, will want to be around her more," promised Nancy Friday in her 1977 bestseller, *My Mother/My Self*. "She must not define herself as 'a mother,' she's got to see herself as a person, a person with work to do, a sexual person, a woman. It isn't necessary to have a profession. She doesn't have to have a high IQ or be president of the PTA to have this added life. So long as she isn't just sitting home, chauffeuring the kids and baking cookies, giving her children and herself the feeling that their life is hers." Wayne Dyer advised, "[I]f you make your children more important than yourself, you are not helping them, you are merely teaching them to put others ahead of themselves, and to take a back seat while remaining unfulfilled. . . . Only by treating yourself as the most important person and not always sacrificing yourself for your children will you teach them to have their own self-confidence and belief in themselves." This teaching found its audience. By the late 1970s, 66 percent of American adults surveyed agreed with the statement "parents should be free to live their own lives even if it means spending less time with their children."

Rising Divorce Rate

Leaving the care of one's children to others became a test of one's commitment to female independence and equality. "Easing the burdens of motherhood and supporting abortion reform are essential tasks, yet they both imply a continuation of a powerless female responsibility for children and for birth control," complained the feminist writer Phyllis Chesler. The National Opinion Research Center found in 1977 that 55 percent of women agreed that "a working mother can establish just as secure and warm a relationship with her child as a mother who does not work." By 1985, 67 percent of women agreed.

In the past, working women had endeavored to place their children in the care of a relative, typically their own mothers. That sense that children whose mothers worked ought at least to be cared for in the family was fading. In 1977, only 13 percent of the children of working mothers attended day-care centers; by 1985 centers took care of 23 percent of the children of a much larger cohort of working mothers. President Nixon vetoed a comprehensive national day-care plan in 1971, but his view that child care was a family responsibility was already obsolete.

It was every bit as important to put oneself first in one's intimate life as in one's worklife. "No marriage should be sustained for the sake of the children," urged a popular divorce book. Once the divorce had occurred, there was no reason to be bashful about one's sexuality. "In my clinical practice, I've found that those single parents who feel good about themselves and have a healthy respect for their own needs are best equipped to be good parents," cooed Mary Mattis, a psychologist who had spent the 1970s counseling divorced women. . . .

In the past, experts had worried about divorce because it undermined the authority of parents. This was just what the new advocates of divorce liked about it. "The multimarriage family can be seen," *The Courage to Divorce* argued, "as an extended kinship system that provides relief from the suffocating relationships children often encounter and endure in the intact nuclear system." After all, the children had to learn to live for themselves too. The divorced single mother was no longer the stern guardian of Puritan morality who so haunted the collective memory of the 1970s. . . .

She was now a friend to her children, almost a sister—just as she was in the 1977–78 television comedy *One Day at a Time*, the first regularly scheduled show to feature a divorced family.

Divorced or married, the parents of the 1970s found it uncomfortable and awkward to exert authority over their children. The boomers who had been raised on the not exactly stern [childcare expert] Dr. Spock turned when their own children arrived to Penelope Leach, an English baby guru whose first book appeared in the United States in 1978. Leach popularized the new child psychology of the era, which held that the word "no" crushes children's fragile self-esteem. It might seem paradoxical that the same era could at once so indulge and so neglect its children. But is it? Indulgence follows neglect as surely as hangovers follow booze. The parents of the 1970s may have been more obsessive about their children than the parents of earlier times, more determined to buy the right educational toys, more frantic about placing them in the right school. But this sort of obsessiveness flows much more from the parent's own ego than from the needs of the child. There was much talk in the 1970s of how male sexual hunger transformed women into objects. Parental obsessiveness can do the same to children. Objects? Some were prepared to venture further still, and treat children as commodities. One of the brightest legal minds of the 1970s, Richard Posner of the University of Chicago, a future Reagan appointee to the Seventh Circuit Court of Appeal, proposed that the chaotic system of adoption be replaced by the straightforward sale and purchase of children. He was only slightly ahead of his time. Twenty years later, the sale and purchase of offspring would become a familiar feature of American life, as sperm banks, egg donors, surrogate mothers, and international adoption enabled those with cash to acquire their dream baby. The fateful step toward this baby market of the future was taken on July 25, 1978, when a healthy six-pound girl was born in Lancashire, England: the first human being to have been conceived in a petri dish.

Chapter 4

Growing Up

Turning|Points

IN WORLD HISTORY

From Hippies to Yuppies

Anthony M. Casale and Philip Lerman

Nineteen-eighty was a watershed year for the baby boom generation as Ronald Reagan was elected president and the Republicans took the White House and the Senate for the first time since the 1950s. Although the seventy-two-year-old Reagan was a member of the World War II generation—and his right-wing conservative politics were diametrically opposed to the Woodstock generation—he found broad support among baby boomers whose views on life were beginning to change as they aged. In the following excerpt, journalists Anthony M. Casale and Philip Lerman discuss how a generation that once praised drugs, sex, and rock and roll transformed itself into money conscious young urban professionals, or yuppies, during the 1980s.

Reagan was swept into office on a platform of tax cuts, decreased power for the federal government, increased power for the states, and a strong national defense. In truth, he was swept into office on the strength of seeming to be the last man in America who genuinely believed in the American Way, who sincerely felt that, by golly, this was a great country, and that if only everyone knew it they would be fine. He was not merely going to preside over the nation; he was going to heal it.

The Reagan Revolution swung into full force almost immediately. He ordered a freeze on federal hiring and government regulations. Then he announced a plan to cut the federal work force and tie welfare to work requirements.

Those who thought he could be tamed—those who thought he would be disastrous for social programs, for the poor, for single mothers, and figured they would be able to shield the neediest from his budget-slashing ax—were stunned at the swiftness with which this old man could move.

They stood by like the bad guys at the bar in one of Reagan's old western movies, and got the smirks wiped off their faces as he whipped out his pistol and fired six perfect shots at them.

Six more shots would ring out soon; fortunately, the aim was not perfect.

On March 30, 1981, Reagan was emerging from the Washington Hilton Hotel, after a speech to union delegates of the AFL-CIO. . . .

Walking out of the hotel through the VIP exit, he raised his arm in that grandfatherly wave. Suddenly he was crumbling, shot in the chest. Press Secretary James Brady was lying on the sidewalk, blood oozing from his head; a police officer lay next to him. A man named John Hinckley was pinned to the ground by Secret Service agents, and the nation prepared for its mourning ritual.

Not again, the nation sighed.

This is how absurd things had become. Someone of the Woodstock generation—Hinckley was thirteen at the time of Woodstock—had tried to assassinate the president. Why? To win the heart of actress Jodie Foster, who had once starred in a movie about a man, driven crazy by life, who plots to shoot a presidential candidate.

But Reagan would not die.

He broke the cycle of America's practiced mourning ritual, adding to his myth, and making him seem bigger than life. His shooting recalled all the other shootings, all the way back to JFK—only this time, the Big Man rewrote the ending.

"I hope you're all Republicans," Reagan quipped to doctors just before they operated to repair the bullet's damage.

"I forgot to duck," he explained to Nancy.

"All in all, I'd rather be in Philadelphia," he jested after surgery.

Here was Reagan, not cynical but grinning at death. Laughing at it!

Somehow, Reagan's survival came to symbolize a renewal of the nation's spirit. And for a generation whose spirit was sorely sagging, a chord was finally struck.

It may have introduced the wrong song—this was not the president who stood for the things people sang about at Woodstock. Nevertheless, Reagan would bring that sense of renewal. These were tough times. Renewal was enough. It was shelter from the storm. . . .

And now Reagan, just a few days after being shot, was cheerily walking out of the hospital, refusing even a wheelchair. The king was well again, the land would be rich again, the crops would grow, and prosperity would be restored.

Becoming a Nation of Believers

The generation not only believed in Ronald Reagan, but desperately needed to believe in him. He would say the homeless were homeless because they wanted to be, and there was almost no hunger, and ketchup was a vegetable—whatever the king said they believed because, after hitting bottom in the Carter years, they needed desperately to.

Well, maybe not the ketchup part. But the Woodstock generation did fall behind the king. It wasn't the issues that were important now, but the sense of confidence and belonging that the generation longed so deeply for. Belonging to something healthy and happy and prosperous and free.

For the first time in four years a majority of Americans polled said they were "generally optimistic" about the nation's future, and the shift was most dramatic among young adults—the Woodstock generation. The number of people who felt that the nation was finally headed in the right direction increased by more than half

It's not that most generation members—or even a slim majority of them—agreed with what Ronald Reagan was saying. But they liked the way he was saying it—the positive style, the optimistic tone, the sense of confidence. In fact, most members of the Woodstock generation, in those same polls, disagreed strongly with Reagan on almost every specific issue facing the nation. Yet they voted for him and thought he was doing a good job. For the first time since Watergate, since the boring years of Gerry Ford, since the depressing years of Jimmy Carter, he gave them an excuse to feel good about something again.

Later, Reagan would become a central figure for activists to rally against. Then the generation would begin to emerge, to once again fight for the causes and issues important to it.

But in the early 80s Reagan was a central figure for the generation to rally behind.

Before you can change the world, you have to believe it's changeable, and the Woodstock generation had stopped believing that long ago. Ironically, its reemergence started with Ronald Reagan's breaking it out of its stupor, replacing its feeling of impotence with one of strength.

National Review saw this as Reagan calling a nation of believers back from the edge of cynicism.

After Reagan's return from the hospital, he gave a televised address to Congress. *National Review* wrote:

"Reagan has had the skill to make his revolution appear to be simple common sense. 'Our government is too big and it spends too much.' Ovation. Massive public support. Four standing ovations from Congress. Reagan's political momentum appears to be irresistible. Peering gloomily over the president's shoulder in the upper-right-hand quadrant of the screen, [House] Speaker (Tip) O'Neill's rotund countenance said it all. The settled assumptions of half a century were being tossed into the wastebasket."

The generation didn't fall behind Reagan en masse. The opposition remained loud and boisterous in those first years.

In *Jules Feiffer's America: From Eisenhower to Reagan,* Feiffer wrote that "Ronald Reagan . . . is how we might like to picture ourselves if we were packaged for a commercial: easy, manly, outrageous, gracious, humble, good-humored, patriotic. Unlike Jimmy Carter, he is very much larger than life. . . . I suspect that we will survive him out of dumb luck. And for a while, at least, we will have learned his lesson: nostalgia is dangerous as a philosophy of government."

After Reagan's first State of the Union message, in January 1982, Democrats responded by challenging his revolution on national television. His tax cuts, his revamping of the government, his proposals to turn over to the states those messy annoyances like food stamps and payments to poor families with dependent children, were a travesty, they said. An embarrassment to a nation that prided itself on caring about the individual.

They said his theme was not happiness but "unfairness"— to the poor, the old, the farmer, the small businessman.

The Democrats brought on regular citizens; one elderly woman said she liked [Depression-era President Herbert] Hoover better than Reagan because "he was blunt and he was what he seemed, and this one is charming and he beguiles you."

He beguiled all right. And the children of the Woodstock era needed some beguiling.

Reagan rolled back environmental protections in the name of jobs, he cut taxes in the name of stimulating the economy, he vetoed housing bills in the name of reducing the deficit, and they ate it up like an Alice B. Toklas [marijuana-laced] brownie, and it made them feel just as good. Hell, better.

And in the coming years, when Reagan delivered on some of his promises, and the economy surged, and unemployment dropped, the nation was practically giddy.

Woodstock to Wall Street

At this point a true change in the Woodstock generation set in. The name for the change wouldn't be coined for a while; it had to evolve.

YAPs, the generation was called at first, for young aspiring professionals. This name did not stick, perhaps because it conjured up an anti-Semitic connotation; it sounded so much like JAPs, a derogatory name, an acronym for Jewish American Princess.

Then came "yumpies," for young upwardly mobile professionals. But that didn't quite do either. Woodstock members were, in truth, not very upwardly mobile. The economic times didn't allow them to move easily above the financial status of their parents. Their parents owned homes and put their children through college; this generation would struggle just to attain the same level.

"Yuppies" was the term that would stick—young urban professionals. Certainly they were young. They appeared to be urban—they were moving back into the cities, renovating old townhouses, gentrifying neighborhoods. And many were professionals—lawyers, journalists, condo converters.

They were also white and heterosexual, which fact spawned the need for terms like buppies (black urban professionals), guppies (gay . . .), puppies (pregnant . . .), and the like.

Shifting Political Priorities

As Americans became more conservative in the 1980s, some believed the baby boomers as a whole had abandoned the liberal political ideals of their youth. In the following excerpt, professor of political science Paul C. Light examines this perceived shift in politics and argues that the baby boomers had not radically altered their views over time.

Trend: The baby boomers became more conservative on gun control.

Facts: In 1975, 20 percent said gun-control legislation was unnecessary; by 1985, the figure was up five percent.

Conclusion: A trend of sorts, but hardly an age of conservatism.

Trend: The baby boomers became more conservative on spending for blacks.

Facts: In 1975, 10 percent said spending on blacks was excessive; in 1985, the figure was 23 percent.

Conclusion: Another trend, but hardly evidence of racism.

Trend: The baby boomers became less tolerant of pornography.

Facts: In 1975, 21 percent said pornography should be illegal in all cases; in 1985, the figure was 30 percent.

Conclusion: Some evidence of change, but still very little support for this kind of censorship.

Trend: The baby boomers stayed steady on defense spending.

Facts: In 1975, 13 percent said defense spending was inadequate; in 1985, the figure was unchanged.

Conclusion: Hardly evidence of support for the Reagan [administration's] defense build-up [during the eighties]. . . .

Trend: The baby boomers took a hard line on crime.

In reality, yuppies formed a very small part of the generation. As in the 60s the cameras followed the relatively small group of hippies so closely that it seemed that all their generation were flower children, that everybody must get stoned; so now the media focused so intensely on this small group that it seemed that the whole generation was yuppi-

---

Facts: In 1975, 57 percent said capital punishment was a necessary weapon in the war on crime; by 1985, the figure was up 25 points to 82 percent. In 1975, 66 percent said the government was not spending enough on crime and that spending was inadequate; in 1985, the number was 67 percent.

Conclusion: The baby boomers have clearly become much tougher toward criminals.

Trend: The baby boomers became more conservative regarding the rights of the accused.

Facts: In 1975, 78 percent said the courts were too lenient; by 1985, the number was up by eight percent.

Conclusion: The baby boomers have always been conservative on this issue.

Trend: The baby boomers became more conservative regarding welfare spending.

Facts: In 1975, 41 percent said welfare spending was excessive; by 1985, the figure was up by seven percent.

Conclusion: A substantial number of baby boomers were skeptical about welfare spending in both periods.

Trend: The baby boomers became more liberal on foreign aid spending.

Facts: In 1975, 74 percent said government was spending too much on foreign aid; by 1985, the number was down to 66 percent.

Conclusion: Hardly much evidence here of a shift back to liberalism, even if the trend is in the right direction.

Paul C. Light, *Baby Boomers.* New York: W.W. Norton, 1988.

fied, that everybody must get cloned.

And yet there was some truth to this. The incredible exposure in the media and in advertising turned the yuppie image into one of success, and thousands of nonupwardly mobile nonprofessionals jumped on board the bandwagon.

By 1984, when a *Newsweek* cover declared it the "Year of the Yuppie," the change had solidified irrevocably.

There would come C.E. Crimmins' *Y.A.P.—The Official Young Aspiring Professional's Fast-Track Handbook*, which noted bits of the jargon this generation created—like "interface," for communicating with another person or a computer. *The Yuppie Handbook* represented a desire in the mass media to chronicle the yuppie movement, and an even more fervent desire by marketers to sell things to it. And did yuppies buy!

Rolexes and condos and answering machines and VCRs and espresso makers and pasta makers and everything from designer cheese for their shelves to designer diapers for their babies. An estimated two million Walkmans were sold in 1981 alone.

A dress code slowly formed—natural fabrics, styled hair and button-downs for men, power suits and pumps for women.

An ethic also slowly formed—one of achieving, striving, and buying. Suddenly everything was work: working hard and working out and working within the system; working mothers and working relationships; working the phone and working the room and working the nightshift. . . .

It was impossible to escape the yuppie influence. The image was everywhere, from news magazines to American Express commercials.

Tripping Through the Sixties

Brad Blanton, a clinical psychologist, watched the change in the Woodstock generation. While many puzzled over the road from hippie to yuppie, he had ideas about why the change was happening and what problems it might produce.

Blanton knew what he was talking about. Now he treated yuppies. Back then he was a hippie.

At the time of Woodstock, Brad Blanton was almost thirty and a veteran of the civil rights movement. He didn't go to the concert; he had a one-year-old daughter and was into being a father then, a traditional role for a man who had lived a fairly untraditional life.

He was born in Virginia and ran away from home and moved to Texas as a teenager. He did acid before he smoked marijuana, did peyote with the Indians, and learned from both. He believed in telling the truth.

The truth got him fired from Miami University in Ohio. Blanton was teaching the cognitive theory of psychology, and teaching a lot of what he learned on LSD: there is a difference between what is actually going on around you and what your ego is telling you is happening.

He began advocating that students take acid and smoke dope, instruction not appreciated at a good . . . school, and he was soon on his way out.

An ashtray that now sits in his office comes from Mendocino, California, where he spent a month living on a school bus after being kicked off campus. It was part of his own [rock and roll tour], six months of traveling around the country in that school bus, with his daughter and wife. Eventually they formed a commune back in Ohio near Antioch. The community lasted four months, and two of the three couples got divorced—"another great attempt to redo the world that didn't work," he said.

But they were wonderful times for him, times of exploration, of liberation, of experience. On acid, he was forming the basis of the therapy he would use later: don't trust your mind, trust your experience. Learn to tell the difference.

"Following the experience" took him to Bear Creek, off Highway 1 near Big Sur in California. About a dozen people were living there, sometimes more. They lived without clothing, swimming in the creek and sunning on the rocks and getting lost in the woods and reading.

The work they did consisted of drawing lots to see who would don clothes that day and walk to the highway and stand with a sign that said, simply, Food. Cars with hippies would stop—they always stopped; this was the early 70s, after all. The hippies offered food and drugs, and they hung out and talked and got stoned for a while. In the evening whoever had drawn the day's duty would trek back to the creek with the daily offerings.

This would seem like panhandling to those who grew up later. But this was not begging; these people were not homeless. This was called sharing, and they were called a family.

And the sharing was an important thing to do. At rallies people would put out their hats and say, "If you have money, give. If you need money, take." And you would take and give money and somehow everyone came out all right.

So the sharing took place, and as the sun sank, Brad, who had drawn the duty that day, trudged back to camp.

"As a matter of honor, as a pledge, we would open up everything and dump it into a pot," Brad says. "All the dope and all the food in one pot, and we'd stir it up and scoop it out and eat it and see what happened.

"Some nights, I don't know what happened. One night I think we had an orgy. I'm not sure. . . .

Tired of Freedom

Years later, sitting in his office in Washington, D.C., speaking with a southern twang, he laughed, loud and hard, the gutteral laugh coming from a deeply remembered experience, deeply remembered joy.

What happened? What happened to all of "Us"? Why did people stop living like that? And for God's sake why did he leave Bear Creek?

"Well, after a while, after I went back and took a shower and put on some clothes, I really felt good," he says. "It does get a little bit old and you get tired of freedom. It's too much work. It's human nature: when you get tired you want to rest."

A popular metaphor of the time was the story of the monkey and the bottle. The way you trap a monkey, the story went, was to find a big bottle, with a neck just wide enough to put a walnut inside. The monkey puts his hand into the bottle, and grabs the walnut. Now he cannot pull his hand out, because while holding the walnut his fist won't fit back out of the neck of the bottle.

That's what happened to Brad Blanton. He got trapped just like the monkey. For him, the walnut was a shower. For others, it was something else, but always something small, some little walnut.

For some of that generation, raised in nice middle-class homes, it would be nothing more than the desire to cop a good, hot, steamy, soapy shower. For others, maybe clean sheets, a good meal.

Once trapped, there would be new needs: a house to keep your shower in, a room for the bed with the clean sheets, a job to make the money to pay for the good meal. And later, a bigger house, a softer bed, a better job.

Walnuts.

Whatever Brad Blanton's walnut, it brought him back, and he framed his doctoral degrees on his wall next to a sign that says "You're only young once, but you can stay immature forever."

People came to him with what were called stress problems, a term that came into vogue in the late 70s. Poor people were crazy; middle-class people had stress.

Stress is the yuppie disease, and Brad Blanton taught yuppies to deal with it through yoga or autogenic relaxation or polarity therapy.

Exercise came into vogue, but yuppies didn't even exercise right. They saw it as one more occasion for competition.

So when Blanton counsels yuppies—lawyers, doctors, journalists—he counsels them based on a key theory: the conflicts of adulthood parallel the conflicts of adolescence.

A Search for Identity

Yuppies are "perennial adolescents," he says, "They want status. They all want to be rich, and they're all very concerned about other people's expectations. They're perennial adolescents, because materialism has allowed people to remain in adolescence for a long time."

In fact, the emergence of the yuppie personality, and the way the generation hooked onto it, revealed a generation in search of an identity in the early 80s.

"If you were working in a . . . law firm and they were making you kiss their ass for seven years before you could even be considered for partner, and you were working seventy,

eighty, ninety hours a week—they got that out of you because they had you sold on the idea that you might not know
who the hell else you were, but by God you knew you were
a lawyer."

That sense of identity, that sense of belonging, had been
missing for generation members since the early 70s. Now
they found that the sense of belonging could be purchased—
by buying into the yuppie image, they were becoming part
of it.

Statistically, yuppies continued to make up a very small
portion of the baby boom; they would be the minority-that-
seemed-like-a-majority, just like their hippie ancestors.
Later in the decade, studies would show that less than 4 percent of all babyboomers would make more than $35,000 a
year. More than a third would earn less than $10,000 a year.
Asked to describe their lives, babyboomers were the most
likely to say their lives were getting harder, least likely to
say they were happy, most likely to say they were having
marital problems.

But the yuppie image, as opposed to the yuppie reality,
became thoroughly pervasive. It formed the new Us and
Them of society. And in Ronald Reagan's America, yuppies
got to perceive themselves, once again, as the Good Guys.

The simplicity of the images we retain—of Reagan revitalizing the country and yuppies revitalizing themselves—
belies the complicated swirl of activity of those first two
years of Ronald Reagan's America. . . .

In a great metaphor for the lingering malaise of the
Carter years, sinkholes in Florida started sucking things back
into the earth. Cottages, imported cars, and campers just
disappeared, sinking from their own weight into a land unable to hold up under the strain any longer.

And one main issue of the 80s continued to grow in
strength and visibility: hundreds of thousands marched at a
nuclear protest in Central Park in June 1982.

"Gee, it's just like Woodstock," many said. But they
were wrong.

At this and other demonstrations of the time, ex-hippie
onlookers expected the rebirth of hope, the rekindling of

the good old liberal spirit of caring and sharing. They saw hundreds of thousands marching against the nuclear arms race, and thought that surely this was a sign, surely the tide had turned.

Surely not.

There were some victories for liberals. In September 1982 the Senate defeated a proposal that would have restricted abortions—but only the most optimistic (and there were a few of those around at the midpoint of Reagan's first term) thought that winning such a battle meant the end of any war.

It was a time of technological explosion. *Time* magazine's Man of the Year was the computer. And Woodstock members, for the first time, started to feel a little old. For it was not they, but their children, who would grasp the new technology and feel comfortable with it.

For every member of the Woodstock generation who tossed a career aside for advancement into the field of computer programming, two were found who thought it a mystic science. To be sure, they put computers into their homes, and learned a few things on it, like how to write a book, but their offspring mastered the science and moved it along.

There were other technological advances of the time, all striking once-familiar chords in the hearts of the generation. The first shuttle launch took place on April 14, 1981, echoing the national pride of the moon landing just before Woodstock. And in the same December week that Dr. William DeVries implanted the first artificial heart in the body of Barney Clark, Charles Brooks, Jr., became the first person executed by lethal injection.

Rising Cocaine Use

A lethal injection also killed John Belushi, one of heroin and cocaine. He was found dead in a rented Hollywood bungalow in March 1982. It would be wrong to call him a hero of the Woodstock generation—in fact, the generation was making few heroes anymore—but he was certainly their darling disaster, their beloved wildman, the king of crazy.

Ever since he had burst from the Chicago comedy scene to national prominence on "Saturday Night Live," Belushi was—well, different. A legion of late-80s comics owed him a debt for the barriers he broke in comedy: not in the topical sense of a Lenny Bruce, but for the sheer energy and dangerous anything-goes edge to his style.

His rubbery face, his ear for dialects, his apparent delight at smashing and screaming his way through sketches, made him frighteningly funny. His audience was wide: his character of Bluto in *Animal House* set the standard for the beer-swilling campus cutup movies of the 80s. His super-hip teaming with Dan Aykroyd as the Blues Brothers had a multiethnic appeal—besides, the music was damned good.

But mostly he was famous on the exploding New York comedy scene. For a while, just before his death, the hippest place to be was anywhere Belushi was doing cocaine.

Cocaine was enjoying its heyday in the early 80s. It was the yuppie drug of choice. It was everywhere, in the workplace, in nightclubs, on airplanes, on Wall Street, in Hollywood. The party was in the men's room stall. Cocaine had the double attraction of making ordinary people feel extraordinarily brilliant, good-looking, alert, exciting, and sexy. Because it was extremely expensive, possessing it was an instant status symbol.

It was the perfect drug for the Woodstock generation's newest incarnation because it didn't make you tune out; it made you feel incredibly plugged in, wired into everything. Even when Richard Pryor nearly killed himself when a free-base cocaine mixture exploded and burned him severely, the generation did little more than laugh (a common joke at the time was to run a Bic lighter along a tabletop, and ask, "What this? Richard Pryor jogging!").

When *Wired*, the book chronicling Belushi's drug use, was published two years later, Belushi's widow, Judy Jacklyn, would be furious at author Bob Woodward. She felt that he had not portrayed the man she knew and loved, but simply told a drug story.

She may have been right. But Woodward, whether by accident or intent, had seized upon the element that would have the most enduring impact.

A jaded generation could not long remain shocked that another of its celebrities had succumbed to drugs. But as the story of Belushi's death unfolded—of the wild parties, of who was and wasn't there, of who stuck that needle into his arm—a pin burst a balloon that had floated over the generation for so long.

It didn't happen right away, but John Belushi's death would be the beginning of the end of the generation's love affair with drugs. Cocaine would remain immensely popular, for a while. But its relatively positive image at this time—a wild, partying image of working hard all day and tooting up all night—would begin to sour for the Woodstock generation.

A drug paranoia, the likes of which hadn't been seen since the generation's youth, would grow. And the generation itself would participate fully in the antidrug movement.

Over the next few years, athletes and celebrities and just plain folks would all do antidrug commercials. Nancy Reagan's Just Say No to Drugs program would swing into full gear.

Some found this refreshing, a healthy sign that the generation was cleaning up its act. Others lamented having to fight the fights of the 60s again, to hear again calls for extremely harsh sentences for the simplest drug possessions—rather than funding for badly needed treatment programs and education. Either way, the furor following John Belushi's death was the beginning of the generation's finally coming to terms with its own drug habit.

Conspicuous Consumption in the 1980s

Myron Magnet

The 1980s will be remembered as a decade when baby boomers first hit their peak earning years. Some made fortunes on Wall Street from leveraged buyouts, junk bonds, and a steadily climbing stock market. In the following 1987 article journalist Myron Magnet discusses the conspicuous consumption of a new class of baby boomer.

Money, money, money is the incantation of today. Bewitched by an epidemic of money enchantment, Americans in the Eighties wriggle in a . . . dance of materialism unseen since the Gilded Age [in the 1890s] or the Roaring Twenties. Under the blazing sun of money, all other values shine palely. And the . . . decade acclaims but one breed of hero: He's the honcho with the condo and the limo and the Miró [painting] and lots and lots of dough.

The evidence is everywhere you turn. Open the scarlet covers of the Saks Fifth Avenue Christmas catalogue, for starters, and look at what Santa offers today's young family, from Dad's $1,650 ostrich-skin briefcase and Mom's $39,500 fur coat to Junior's $4,000, 15-mph miniature Mercedes, driven by a 5-year-old Donald Trump look-alike in pleated evening shirt, studs, and red suspenders. Take a stroll along Manhattan's Madison Avenue and gape at the Arabian Nights' bazaar of shop windows, where money translates life's commonest objects into rarities rich and strange. Behold embroidery encrusted sheets fine enough for the princess and the pea, or ladies' shoes as fanciful and elaborate as any that artisans painstakingly toiled over when [18th century French Queen] Marie Antoinette graced the throne, or sumptuous lace underwear that makes the inconspicuous yet another arena for conspicuous consumption and adds the charm of wealth to the ordinariness of seduction. Visit Bijan, the temple of excess on Rodeo Drive and Fifth Avenue [in Los Angeles], and pick up five matched crocodile suitcases for $75,000—yes, thousand—perhaps to be filled with business shirts at $550 and $650 apiece.

Statistics tell the same glitzy story as the evidence of your senses. Luxury car imports more than doubled between 1982 and 1986, while the average age of the growing hordes of first-time fur coat owners has fallen from a matronly 50 to a yuppier 26 in ten years. An overwhelming 93% of recently surveyed teenage girls deemed shopping their favorite pasttime, way ahead of sixth-rated dating. Back in 1967, around 40% of U.S. college freshmen told pollsters that it was important to them to be well off financially, as against around 80% who listed developing a meaningful philosophy of life as an important objective. But by 1986 the numbers had reversed, with almost 80% aspiring plutocrats as against 40% philosophers. The number and wealth of the rich have swollen accordingly, with U.S. millionaires proliferating sixfold over the last 20 years to around 1.3 million souls today. The richest 1% of Americans, who owned 31.8% of the national wealth in 1963, had upped their share to an even heftier 34.4% of it two decades later.

But you needn't be rich to catch the money fever—as witness those 26 million middle-class Americans, mostly earning under $40,000 a year, who treat themselves to such badges of affluence as $380 Burberry raincoats and $200 Mont Blanc pens, in the process raising consumer debt to its highest level ever. Their children have the bug too: in many high schools, they roll up to the senior prom in limousines, rented at $250 for the night. So many high schoolers work such long hours at after-school jobs that teachers have been going easier on homework assignments. "Saving for college?" you ask approvingly. Nope. Most of these earnings go for stereos, cars, trendy clothes, and the other material trappings of modern kid life.

Obsessing About Money

As the stock market roared upward in the 1920s, securities and investing turned from being topics not discussed before ladies to the centerpieces of the politest dinner table conversation. Today we obsessively talk about money almost nonstop: how much they paid for their house, their boat, their painting; how big the deal was; how much this one makes—and that one and that one. We read about it too, not just in Judith Krantz sex-and-shopping novels but in magazines that author Tom Wolfe lumps together as *plutography*, the graphic depiction of the acts of the rich. Peep into their windows in *Architectural Digest*, admire their indulgences in *Town & Country* or *Connoisseur*, eavesdrop on their gossip in *Vanity Fair*. Or tune in to the same fare on TV, from the wildly successful *Lifestyles of the Rich and Famous* to the goings-on of their fictional counterparts on *Dallas* or *Dynasty* and its clones. Says veteran Washington hostess Oatsie Charles: "It's hard for the young to realize how much things have changed. I don't remember in my lifetime being so conscious of money."

And what people won't do for it. Forget about televangelists Jim and Tammy Bakker and their squandered millions: Magnified by TV, they've only expanded on an old American tradition, rather than inventing something new. But John Walker Jr., the spy, seems entirely an emanation of our own age. Previous spies . . . turned traitors out of conviction, however contemptibly deluded. Walker, by contrast, corrupted his family and betrayed his country for nothing but money. And what about wellborn Sydney Biddle Barrows, the Mayflower Madam? Add to vice a dash of marketing flair and managerial skill, and—poof—you're an entrepreneurial culture hero like [Apple Computer founder] Steven Jobs, welcome at the dinner tables of the fashionable and selling as many entrepreneur's-true-confessions books as a more upstanding competitor like [Dallas billionaire] T. Boone Pickens.

Laughing All the Way to the Bank

All this, however, isn't a call to repent for the end is nigh. Modern materialism doesn't mean that America is hopelessly mired in corruption, despite some luminous instances of it, including those on Wall Street. A portion of the money furor has a healthy impulse at its base, and most of it grows naturally out of big changes in American life. Some of the excesses of the money craze will moderate as the circumstances causing them shift. Others are deeply rooted in the basic facts of modern life—and it's there that you'll have to look if you seek to change them.

In an earlier age, a whole generation had its attitudes, its very feelings, formed by the Depression. Though a much less spectacular or painful event, the inflation of the Seventies similarly sank into the marrow of many Americans. Saving and shunning debt was for saps, the lesson seemed to be; buy, buy, buy, before the money visibly crumbling to dust in your hand vanishes completely. Harvard Business School Professor Samuel Hayes III describes what happened to one of his elderly relatives: "He was the epitome of the Protestant ethic. He had inherited money, he had saved, he was very frugal, had a very modest house, had part of his investment money in bonds and short-term securities, had always maintained liquidity. And he came out of the Seventies looking like a fool. The people who had frittered away their money, as he would say, on elaborate homes and material possessions were laughing all the way to the bank."

Not just economic values but also moral ones got turned upside down by the inflation, in other words, and in the process the moral and the economic orders seemed to pull apart. . . .

People who had bought houses simply for shelter suddenly found themselves much richer than their neighbors who hadn't. That, along with the fortunes made by more calculating speculators, led many to feel that, as in a lottery, one's economic fate bore little relation to one's hard work or self-denial or contribution to human well-being. Compounding the sense of the injustice of the economic order was the spectacle of a [Arab oil billionaire] Sheik Yamani lecturing the West on discipline and restraint, while his countrymen, inflation's accessories and No. 1 beneficiaries, gorged on every luxury that only the West and Japan had the skill and industry to produce.

Europeans might have turned resentful. Americans had a different, purely American, response. Says James Kouzes, director of Santa Clara University's Executive Development Center: "When other people are achieving certain things, you feel, 'How come not me? I'm entitled.' Some of the feeling of entitlement comes from the feeling that we all ought to be treated fairly." The practical expression of that sense of entitlement turned out to be a sharper money hunger and materialism.

Don't forget that inflation made these impulses eminently realistic. You had to wonder whether you would have the things you had always expected to be able to earn—a home, college for your kids, a non-poorhouse retirement. Kouzes, for instance, says he couldn't afford to buy from his mother the suburban Washington house he grew up in—a house his father had afforded on a mid-level civil servant's income. "So," says he, "it's real hard not to focus on making a lot more than I'm now making."

Grab It While You Can

What inflation started in the Seventies, the corporate restructuring of the Eighties completed. However necessary for improving U.S. competitiveness in a newly global marketplace, the plant closings and headquarters shutdowns, the give-backs and two-tier wage scales imposed on production workers, the purges of middle managers that followed bust-ups, mergers, and slim-downs—all these stunned not only victims but also survivors, suffusing them with insecurity. Every man for himself was the implicit message; if you don't look out for No. 1, you can bet no one else will. Certainly not the top guys in your company: Spurred by their own fear of takeover, they often seem too busy protecting their own interests to attend to yours or the corporation's.

Young people, in particular, took this lesson to heart. Roderick Gilkey, a psychologist who teaches management at the Emory Business School in Atlanta, says that students who are children of purged managers have been especially anxious to go out and make as much money as they can, to ensure a cushion for the hard times they see as inevitable.

But even in students personally unaffected by the restructuring he sees a "desperate, worried flight to get on the train before it leaves—a sort of window-of-opportunity mentality that you've got to grab it while you can."

Part of what makes the materialism of the Eighties different from that of the Fifties is this edge of anxiety. Says Senior Vice President Ann Clurman of the Yankelovich Clancy Shulman market research firm: "The 1950s sense was, 'If I play by all the rules, I'll make it up the economic ladder rung by rung.' Now it's more like, 'I'm not sure I'm going to win even if I play by all the rules.'"

Meanwhile, watching the investment bankers who preside over the restructuring wallow so conspicuously in money, observers feel the same sense of unfairness and entitlement they felt when speculators made fortunes from the inflation of the Seventies. Whether they think, wrongly, that the restructuring is nothing but unproductive paper shuffling or, more accurately, that [government banking rules] gives investment bankers a windfall that a free market would withhold, they perceive the fees as undeserved—whereas they don't begrudge Steven Jobs his fortune, earned by producing something of tangible value. Under the slightly Frankensteinian toupee of junk bond alchemist Michael Milken, they know, bubbles a redoubtable brain; but is it an organ worth the half billion dollars it has earned? They doubt it. And discovering that insider trading has helped make some of the Wall Street money only fans their sense of inequity and entitlement.

The corporate restructuring isn't just an economic change. It is also a social change, transforming the relationships between individuals and their employers. Altered sometimes unrecognizably, cut loose from their traditions, no longer able to offer long-term career commitment, old companies can inspire neither attachment nor loyalty in employees. "What we're living in now is an age of Hessians [mercenaries]," says University of Rhode Island historian Maury Klein, biographer of robber baron Jay Gould. A realignment like this cuts people adrift from the traditional moorings by which they identify themselves, as do other of our era's social and cultural changes, from family breakdown to the newfangled relations between the sexes to the continuing attenuation of community ties.

What has this to do with the money craze? Everything. Says historian Klein, "Money tends to be more or less important in an age, depending on the degree of turbulence and social change that is taking place." Like the rapidly urbanizing and industrializing era of the robber barons [in the late 19th century], Klein says, ours is "an age where traditional self-identities are under great attack and great strain just from the pace of change. In that situation, money becomes a way of defining who you are by what you have."

Stress and Turmoil

That way of defining a self is rampant in the money society. Classic cases seem shoulder to pin-striped shoulder on Wall Street, where it's worth looking for the full-blown symptoms of a malady widespread in the society as a whole. "Wall Streeters heavily look on their self-worth by their W-2," says the vice president in charge of compensation at a major Wall Street firm. And they look at others that way, too. "I think people are being measured again by money rather than by how good a journalist or social activist or lawyer they are," says an investment banker at a prestigious New York firm. Explains one representative Wall Streeter, a managing director in the corporate finance wing of a major commercial bank: "What differentiates you and says you're successful is the house in the Hamptons and the Ferrari in the driveway."

As a result, this banker is continually comparing himself with others to make sure he's okay. He schmoozes about compensation to try to determine if he makes more or less than the person he's talking to. But such conversations can be inconclusive, so when he visits friends or business acquaintances he's continually sizing up the towels, the cars, the silver, with practically an auctioneer's eye to see what he's worth by comparison. Told by his wife that friends were drinking out of Baccarat glasses, more expensive than his Waterford ones, he demanded to know why she hadn't bought Baccarat, too.

"It frightens me to be sensitive to the idea that my neighbor just got a big-screen TV that's three inches bigger than mine," says the banker. "But that's something I look at. Or I know the guy got $100,000 more in his compensation package last year than I did. Why should that bother me? Can I spend it? Do I need it? Do I want it? Only because I want to make more than him. I think the stress and internal turmoil that creates in most of us is unhealthy."

For this is an endless and unwinnable competition, even on purely economic terms. Says Harvard professor of political economy Robert Reich: "When everybody is buying into the same status objects, such as the house in the Hamptons or the co-op on the East Side, they balloon in price, so it costs more and more to achieve relative status. it becomes a fruitless exercise after a while. That is part of the cycle of disillusionment that sets in." Out of this phenomenon came a recent, and notorious, *New York Times* story about investment bankers feeling poor on $600,000 a year—a story that investment bankers, without irony, earnestly assure you is true.

More important, this is an unwinnable game psychologically. Like an addiction, it requires higher and higher doses for the same thrill. Psychoanalysts find that many money addicts are children of parents too preoccupied, overworked, or withdrawn to respond with the appropriate oohs and ahs to baby's smiles and antics. The children consequently never stop looking for the withheld applause and pleased response, and money helps them get it—even takes the place of it, as a sign of the employer's pleasure and approval. But, says Dr. Arnold Goldberg, a Chicago psychoanalyst, "The ante always goes up because the need is never satisfied. The kid wants a human response; money is a nonhuman response." Some of these people, rich and successful, end up in Goldberg's office complaining that their life has no purpose. Worse, those cashoholics who fail to get their needed infusion of money, according to Dr. Jay Rohrlich, a psychiatrist with offices in the heart of Wall Street, become agitated, anxious, combative, and depressed, like addicts deprived of their fix.

Trouble is, money is only money. "There's a kind of bewilderment over what sources can be drawn upon to provide money with a sense of distinction, purpose, or value," says

Hilton Kramer, editor of *The New Criterion*, a cultural review. The very rich have a smorgasbord of strategies. There's the high society route. Says Lazard Frères partner Felix Rohatyn: "Today you can essentially buy social status immediately, with all the trimmings." That's because in the Eighties the old rich increasingly seem to take their cue from the new rich, rather than vice versa. Presumably that's because they like the glamour and glitz. "Social status today involves an enormous amount of publicity and a certain level of stardom," says Rohatyn. "We've become Beverly Hills."

Or you can try to cloak yourself in the authority and solidity of the old regime. Here on the cover of the home entertaining section of the *New York Times Magazine* is dress designer Carolyn Roehm, wife of investment banker Henry Kravis of Kohlberg Kravis Roberts, the leveraged buyout kings. In sweeping floor-length gown, she's just getting ready for a dinner party for 18 in an opulent dining room so perfect in every detail of its superb antique furniture and breathtaking 18th- and 19th-century paintings that it looks like a stage set or a model room in a museum. Add to this that she's displaying it all on a magazine cover and vaporing inside about how "in college, when traditions went asunder, we all dined in blue jeans on the floor," and you can't help thinking that while some girls play house, this lady is playing castle. On a more demotic level, the . . . clothes and advertisements of designer Ralph Lauren, along with his baronial New York store in a mansion refurbished to look as if the original tycoon still lives there, have the same intent of using the outward trappings of a vanished order to appropriate its rootedness and dignity.

Finally, there's the way of art. "In this whole materialist explosion, an interest in art represents an interest in spirit," says Hilton Kramer. So urgent is this spiritual interest that the prices of paintings have rocketed in the last five years, with a Jasper Johns recently selling for $3.6 million. Some dignitaries of the money society buy pictures because of the status art confers; others really get to care about it.

What then is one to make of that patron of the arts Saul Steinberg, chairman of Reliance Group Holdings . . . recently host to a gathering of such writers as Norman Mailer and Allen Ginsberg? . . .

Money Counts

All this is what is really meant by the word "lifestyle"—more superficial style than rooted, meaningful life. And the point of these examples is not that the money society has triumphantly driven out all the solid, estimable values, like the shaggy barbarians at the gates of Rome. Rather, the money society has expanded to fill the vacuum left after the institutions that embodied and nourished those values—community, religion, school, university, and especially family—sagged or collapsed or sometimes even self-destructed.

Now we live in a world where all values are relative, equal, and therefore without authority, truly matters of mere style. Says Dee Hock, former chief of the Visa bank-card operation: "It's not that people value money more but that they value everything else so much less—not that they are more greedy but that they have no other values to keep greed in check. They don't know what else to value." Or as University of Pennsylvania sociologist E. Digby Baltzell puts it: "When there are no values, money counts."

Editorialists who recently have been haranguing the young to give up all this soulless materialism and return to the commitment of the Sixties have got it exactly wrong. That "commitment," with its heavy charge of destructive anger and protest, ultimately helped bleed the value out of existing institutions, giving them their present zombielike character. Many who chose the materialist life were consciously rejecting the Sixties and their legacy of destructiveness and nihilism. They were trying to choose the solid bourgeois existence of home and hearth and work that the Sixties had jeered down as worthless. But after the mutilation of so many of the values that in the past had given that life its meaningfulness and security, many who opted for it discovered that little more than an empty shell was left for them. That this life should end up being only one more "lifestyle" is really what the problem of the money society is all about.

Computers: Another Kind of Revolution

Michael Gross

While a vocal group of baby boomers were trying to fo-
ment political rebellion during the late 1960s a small group
of hackers spent their time liberating proprietary computer
information in hopes of bringing about a communications
revolution. As reporter and best-selling author Michael
Gross writes, by the 1980s, this motley group of former
war protesters, hippies, Yippies, and even LSD chemists,
were responsible for laying the foundation of the modern
digital revolution, changing the world forever by making
personal computers widely available to the general public.

The computer revolution had begun in the late 1950s. At
that time, there was only one paradigm for computer use.
Manufacturers like IBM, Digital Equipment Corporation,
Wang and Data General sold black boxes—huge mainframe
computers with magic inside. "We're the priests with the
keys to the temple; you've got to come to the priests," [com-
puter pioneer John] Gage says, satirizing the prevailing proprietary attitude. At MIT, computer aficionados (for there
was no computer science department yet) began attempting
to improve the software that ran the school's multimillion-
dollar IBM mainframe computer. They called themselves
"hackers," and though they seemed worlds away from the
dope-smoking, anti-logic radicals then coming of age on less
technocratic campuses, they had the equally radical idea that
the keys to the temple of computing should be freely available to anyone, not only those approved by the priests. Indeed, they felt that all information should be free, so it might
be shared and bettered.

From *My Generation: Fifty Years of Sex, Drugs, Rock, Revolution, Glamour, Greed,
Valor, Faith, and Silicon Chips*, by Michael Gross. Copyright © 2000 by Michael
Gross. Used by permission of HarperCollins Publishers, Inc.

In the early 1960s, the hackers got their hands on the tool that would wrest computing from the priests forever—the minicomputer. Though they were as big as refrigerators at first, these machines were revolutionary: unlike huge room-size mainframes, they were accessible, nimble and inspiring to those who didn't want to put on white shirts and ties and join IBM's army of bureaucrats. By the 1970s, computer science and the hacker ethic had spread across the country. Computers offered a safe haven of logic in an increasingly il-logical world. For students on the run from the collapsing 1960s youth culture, computer culture was a godsend. Here was something they could control.

The Early Internet

In the Bay Area, schools like Stanford and Berkeley formed the vanguard of the cyberrevolution. Beginning in 1969, they were all hooked up to a Defense Department-funded network called ARPAnet. ARPA, the Advanced Research Projects Agency, had been funding computer research since the end of World War II, investing about a billion dollars on advanced projects to make a better military. . . . But ARPA also funded pure computer research, allowing hackers to take its money without the slightest guilt. At MIT and Stan-ford, some ARPA money was even spent developing early computer games like Spacewar and Adventure.

The ARPAnet was developed to make the most of scarce computing resources by connecting users and resources, even at a great distance, but it soon turned into a communi-cations medium as academics, technical types and an avant-garde of ex-hippies, science fiction aficionados and anar-chists began connecting through a new technology called electronic mail. ARPAnet was based in "the belief that sys-tems should be decentralized, encourage exploration, and urge a free flow of information," Steven Levy wrote in *Hack-ers*, a history of the computer revolution. Similar values had driven the now-waning youth movement.

Key computer research was also taking place at Bell Labs, the phone company's scientific arm, which developed a com-puter operating system called Bell UNIX. . . .

Bill Joy was one of the student programmers who dug into the program, creating a version known as Berkeley UNIX. In 1980, Joy rewrote a set of standards (computer instructions written in code) known as TCP/IP networking protocols, which systematized communication between computers on the ARPAnet. Without TCP/IP, "you could be getting it all but not understanding a word I'm saying," explains Gage, who by 1982 was working with Joy on Berkeley's computing strategy. "Bill put the new protocols out free on the Internet—very Berkeley—and everybody took his code and made their computers work. He became the God of Internet-distributed computing. Anybody in the world could now be in the conversation." A year later, the Domain Name Service came into being, a sort of cyberspace city planning agency, and the word *Internet* started being used in place of ARPAnet.

As the Internet was being born, a separate group of computer boomers was creating the computer revolution's other essential component: cheap hardware. While Gage was working on the McGovern campaign, a group called Community Memory was installing a public computer terminal, open to anyone, near a record store in Berkeley. In 1971 a science fiction fan named Lee Felsenstein (b. 1945), who'd been arrested at Sproul Hall on December 2, 1964 [in the first college protest of the sixties], and then joined the staff of the underground newspaper *Berkeley Barb*, gained access to his first computer.

Felsenstein was one of the pioneers—many of them former activists—of what would soon coalesce into a populist movement to bring computing power to the people. All over the Bay Area, others were having the same idea, and by 1975, the first commercially available PC, a bare-bones affair called Altair 8800, based on a new microprocessor chip made by a Santa Clara company, Intel, was made available in hobby kit form (although without any programs or input devices like keyboards or mice). On March 5, 1975, two computer kit enthusiasts held the first meeting of the Homebrew Computer Club at one of their homes in Menlo Park. Within four months, the meetings had grown so large, they had to be held in an auditorium at Stanford. In June, Felsenstein started chairing those meetings.

Among those frequenting Homebrew—sharing information, advances, and even code, as required by the tenets of hackerism—were engineers from Hewlett-Packard, including shaggy-haired Steve Wozniak (b. 1940), often accompanied by a high school friend just back from a hippie trek to India and a spell in an Oregon commune, Steve Jobs (b. 1945). Jobs was working for Atari, which was then developing a computerized game called Pong. In college, Jobs and Woz, as he was known, had built and sold blue boxes, illegal devices that let users make free long distance calls. Now, inspired by Homebrew, Wozniak set out to build his own computer. By that winter, it was done, and Jobs, dazzled by his friend's invention, insisted they build and sell them. Financed by the sale of Jobs's Volkswagen bus, they incorporated in spring 1976. Jobs, who was proud of his hippie roots and often went barefoot, named the company Apple after the Beatles' record label. Meanwhile, Wozniak created a new machine, the Apple II, which would include a color terminal. It wasn't as advanced as the Xerox Alto, but at least you could buy an Apple.

From Prison to PCs

Tim Scully had a plan to use his time in prison [after an arrest for making large amounts of LSD] to earn a doctoral degree and continue the psycho-electronic explorations he'd started while out on bail. In 1974, just after his release on appeal bond, Intel had introduced its 8008 chip, the key component in microcomputers. Scully built a physiological monitoring system around one for use in drug and alcohol rehabilitation programs. Then, when Intel's 8080 chip followed in 1975, he built a computer to detect and record changes in consciousness in biofeedback sessions.

He'd introduced himself to the prison's psychological services staff at McNeil Island during his first sojourn there and corresponded with them while he was out on bail, in the hope they'd allow him to set up a biofeedback program when he returned. He was afraid prison would be full of the sort of guys who'd beaten him up in high school. Instead, he arrived with a rep as a drug czar who didn't rat, and his worst problem was convincing inmates he couldn't sell them acid. But after he got an inmate job as an assistant to one of the resident psychologists, he *could* get them high, help them relax, and combat stress—with biofeedback.

While out on bail, Scully had met a woman suffering from cerebral palsy who could only communicate by laboriously pointing out letters one at a time to her parents with a telegraph key attached to her knee. After he'd been at McNeil a year, Scully got permission to build her a microcomputer and program it using principles of cryptography, allowing the young woman to communicate up to thirty times faster, and later, to write and print out notes and essays. It was so successful, he began building them for other disabled people, adding extensions that controlled devices from page-turners to light switches. When inexpensive speech synthesizers came on the market, he added those, too, so users could have their messages read out loud. Federal Prison Industries took note and began a program to build the machines and offer them to speech-impaired veterans. Though the costs of customizing the device and gaining necessary approvals made the project unfeasible, years later, Scully rewrote the program for PCs and distributed it free on the Internet. The project won him an award as 1979's Outstanding Young Man of the Year from the Washington Jaycees, which had a chapter inside the prison.

Scully was indeed an outstanding prisoner. "My first priority was to stay out of trouble with the inmate population, because the penalty could be death," he says. "Second was to stay out of trouble with the staff. After that, I just wanted not to rot away." He taught classes in computer design, programming and tai chi to fellow inmates, and wrote a dissertation on his biofeedback experiments, earning a Ph.D. He also won a sentence reduction. In August 1979, he was released to a halfway house in San Francisco. . . .

Steve Wozniak was a believer in the hacker ideal. While he was working on the Apple, a competing idea entered the PC Garden of Eden and was quickly condemned as an unmitigated evil. Initially, the first small computer, the Altair, was shipped without an operating system. Then two computer-savvy friends from Seattle, Paul Allen (b. 1953) and Bill Gates (b. 1955), co-founders of what would become the software behemoth Microsoft, heard about the Altair and offered to create a basic program to run it. It was called Altair BASIC, modeled on the clunky but easy-to-use BASIC programming language developed at Dartmouth in the 1960s, and subsequently championed by the People's Computer Company in Berkeley and its founder, Bob Albrecht. Albrecht . . . was the Johnny Appleseed of West Coast computing, and BASIC was his seed.

After Allen successfully sold the program to Altair, Gates dropped out of Harvard and began to debug—or perfect—it. Unfortunately, Altair's manufacturer had already started shipping machines without BASIC, so members of Homebrew, who'd gotten hold of an earlier version, started copying it and giving it away for free, as hackers had done since the 1960s. Gates, already working on versions for other microcomputer brands, was furious. His dream was "a computer on every desk and in every home, (all) running Microsoft software." This copying was a bad start. In an act that would reverberate for decades to come, Gates, then nineteen, wrote a widely circulated "Open Letter to Hobbyists," pleading with them to stop stealing his software. "Who can afford to do professional work for nothing?" Gates wrote. The Homebrew hackers dismissed him as a whiner.

From then on, the computing world broke down into two competing (if sometimes overlapping) camps, a war between two Baby Boom paradigms. On one side were post-hippies like Wozniak, Gage, Felsenstein and Joy, still openly idealistic. On the other were the new vanguard, folks like the software tycoon Gates, who believed in profit-making, proprietary, closed-model computing. Somewhere in the middle were the Apple crew, who played both ends against the middle, acting tastefully hip while they sold a proprietary hardware system (Jobs won out over Wozniak on that score).

At first, the big computer companies couldn't have cared less. Hewlett-Packard, for instance, had turned down Wozniak when he brought his Apple design to them. In 1977, major corporations like Commodore and Radio Shack began marketing microcomputers. It wasn't until fall 1979, though, that . . . VisiCalc, a spreadsheet or accounting program written for the Apple II by a Harvard Business School student named Dan Bricklin (b. 1951), went on the market. It was the so-called "killer app" that introduced first thousands, then millions of people to computing. The spreadsheet was followed by word processors. "With that combination," Gage says, "the little ugly box on your desk became useful."

By 1980, Apple was earning more than $100 million a year and poised to go public.

Chapter 5

Growing Old

Turning|Points
IN WORLD HISTORY

Strains of an Aging Population

William Sterling and Stephen Waite

The first wave of baby boomers turned fifty-five in 2001. With retirement looming on the horizon for nearly 76 million people in the following two decades, America's social security and health care institutions will be pushed to the limit as fewer taxpayers are forced to fund medical care and social services for this aging section of the population. Investment strategists William Sterling and Stephen Waite take a look at the numbers and explain what it will mean to American society as a whole as millions of healthy baby boomers eventually turn into ailing senior citizens.

There is still more than a decade before boomers start to retire in large numbers, but confidence in the nation's Social Security system is slipping badly. The Social Security Advisory Council recently fretted about "unprecedentedly low levels of confidence" in Social Security. In fact, a 1994 survey revealed that more young Americans believe in UFOs than believe they will ever receive a dime in Social Security benefits. Countless articles and news programs about how the financing of Social Security resembles an unsustainable chain letter have undoubtedly sunk in.

We're not sure about UFOs, but we have little doubt that the enormously popular Social Security program will be "fixed" one way or another in coming years. Benefits will be cut, payroll taxes will be raised, and the age for receiving benefits will probably be pushed back toward seventy. A national debate is already under way on how to fix the huge gap in Social Security's long-term finances, and leaders of both political parties are under pressure to come up with a credible solution.

From *Boomernomics* by William Sterling and Stephen Waite. Copyright © 1998 by William P. Sterling and Stephen R. Waite. Used by permission of Ballantine Books, a division of Random House, Inc.

The myth is that Social Security is the third rail of domestic politics—touch this popular program and you're dead. The truth is that politicians of both parties have already performed a line dance on the third rail and gotten away relatively unscathed. This occurred in 1983, when Congress enacted legislation effectively reducing the present value of baby boomers' Social Security benefits by a whopping $1.2 trillion. This was done through relatively stealthy means—the retirement age for most boomers was increased from sixty-five to sixty-seven, benefit levels were cut for those who retired early, and certain benefits were suddenly subject to the taxman's axe. . . .

Since most baby boomers in 1983 were then naïfs in their twenties or early thirties, it is not surprising that the gray eminences in Congress were able to cut their future benefits with little outcry.

Bankruptcy Ahead

Now that the boomers themselves are sprouting gray hairs, the debate about their retirement benefits is likely to be somewhat more serious. Led by Boomer-in-Chief Bill Clinton, baby boomers are more politically engaged than they were in the 1980s. Boomer politicians now make up a majority in the House of Representatives. . . . So there is a good chance that such stealth measures to "fix" the Social Security system will be announced in the next few years. At the very minimum, these measures should . . . push out the projected date—which is currently 2032—when its combined trust funds go bankrupt.

There is even serious talk of the government investing some of the dubiously named Social Security Trust Fund in the [stock] market. . . .

That said, we shudder to think about all the political shenanigans that would eventually flow from making Uncle Sam a large direct shareholder in almost every major American corporation.

Even better, there is growing support for moving in the direction of partly privatizing Social Security. That would let Americans control some of their Social Security payroll taxes themselves, in private mutual funds, instead of seeing them disappear into the black hole of the Social Security "Trust" Fund. In our opinion, this would be a crucial step in the right direction. Not only would it bring the entire Social Security system under greater public scrutiny, it would also give most boomers a chance for much higher returns. . . .

Tip of the Iceberg

The problem is that the Social Security system, which is currently the object of so much attention, is merely the tip of the iceberg. According to economists who've studied the numbers carefully, Social Security represents only about 15 percent of the fiscal problems associated with the coming

---

The Baby Boomer Economy

As the baby boomers entered their fifties in the early twenty-first century, they earned a combined $2 trillion in annual income. And although they made up only 27 percent of the population, they controlled more than 70 percent of all financial assets in the United States. In the excerpt below, best-selling author and financial forecaster Ken Dychtwald lists the incredible wealth held by this large demographic group.

Today's *new* mature consumers:

- Control more than $7 trillion in wealth—70 percent of the total
- Own 77 percent of all financial assets
- Comprise 66 percent of all stockholders
- Own 40 percent of all mutual funds ($1 trillion)
- Own almost 60 percent of all annuities
- Represent 50 percent of IRA and Keogh holders
- Own their own homes—over 79 percent of all 50+, by far the highest rate of any age group
- Own 46 percent of home equity loans
- Transact more than 5 million auto loans each year
- Purchase 42 percent of all homeowner's insurance (50 million policyholders)
- Own 38 percent of all life insurance—a $90 billion industry

age wave. Fifteen percent is just about how much of an ice-berg is visible from above the water.

Not surprisingly, the big money is going to be in rising expenses for health care when the boomers retire. According to the pension-consulting firm Watson Wyatt, "The aging of the baby boom generation will deal a staggering blow to the U.S. health care system." Everyone who becomes eligible for Social Security on the basis of age eventually becomes eligible for Medicare as well, with Medicare enrollment expected to increase from its current 14 percent of the population to 22 percent in 2030. With costs per enrollee also escalating rapidly, Medicare spending as a percentage of GDP [Gross Domestic Product] is expected to rise from

- Purchase more than 90 percent of long-term care insurance, representing $800 million in annual premiums—a figure that's growing at 23 percent per year
- Comprise 35 percent of the auto insurance market (50 million consumers)
- Represent 40 million credit card users, owning almost half of the credit cards in the U.S.
- Purchase 41 percent of all new cars (they're much less likely than their younger counterparts to buy used cars) and 48 percent of all luxury cars, totaling more than $60 billion
- Represent more than $610 billion per year in direct healthcare spending
- Account for 51 percent of all over-the-counter drug purchases
- Consume 74 percent of all prescription drugs, a $103 billion market
- Represent 65 percent of all hospital bed days, 42 percent of all physician's office visits, 1.5 million residents in nursing homes, and 1.5 million residents in continuing-care retirement and assisted-living residences.

Ken Dychtwald, *Age Power: How the Twenty-First Century Will Be Ruled by the New Old.* New York: Penguin Putnam, 1999.

around 2 percent now to between 7 and 8 percent in the 2030–2050 period.

Despite all the focus on a Social Security fix, potential problems financing Medicare and Medicaid are currently being swept under the rug. So voters must not allow politicians to become too self-congratulatory about dealing with Social Security or running federal budget surpluses in the next few years. Instead they should be asking, *"How will we fix Social Security, Medicare, and Medicaid on a combined basis?"* and, even more important, *"How much will we need to tax our children?"*

Unfortunately, most credible projections of the combined effects of the age wave on America's expensive social programs show the good ship *America* steaming toward an iceberg. As on the good ship *Titanic*, the decision makers on the top deck are currently enjoying wine, women, and song. Lulled into complacency by the good life and smooth sailing, they are not about to be seriously bothered by reports of danger ahead from worrywart technicians.

And the technicians are definitely worried. Consider, for example, a March 1997 report by the Congressional Budget Office (CBO) with the harmless-sounding title "Long-term Budgetary Pressures and Policy Options." Using the gray language of budget bureaucrats, the report recaps the sobering facts of the age wave: fewer workers to support growing numbers of retirees, growing expenditures for Social Security and Medicare, and so on. . . .

The CBO report then plugs in reasonable estimates for how much Social Security and health care expenses will rise as the boomers age, and grinds out various scenarios for the economy over the first half of the next century. These scenarios assume that no major changes are made to the current relatively generous benefit programs. The results are startling.

Virtually every scenario shows a manageable situation during the next decade, when the boomers remain gainfully employed. Responding to recent data showing a better-than-expected budget outcome for 1997, the report notes that "the improved short-term budgetary outlook brightens the long-term picture" and that recent changes "delay any serious trouble for about seven to ten years.". . .

But here's what the CBO has to say about the . . . period *after* the boomers retire in large numbers:

> Under an array of scenarios with economic feedbacks that assume no change in current budget policy, the debt would increase to historically unprecedented levels in the next four decades. Moreover, as federal debt pushed up interest rates and lowered the growth of the economy, interest payments would begin to consume an ever-larger share of federal spending and eventually grow at an explosive rate. In the end, the total amount of debt held by the public would reach levels that the economy could clearly not support.

Translation: As the boomers swamp the government social safety nets, the budget deficit will explode, bond and stock markets will collapse, and living standards will plummet. It's your basic financial apocalypse. . . .

As the CBO points out: "Policymakers would certainly take the necessary steps to limit the growth of debt before it reached unthinkable levels. But because debt can quickly snowball out of control, policymakers would need to act well before it reached a critical level."

So we all can rest assured. Adjustments will be made. Steps will be taken. Whew! . . .

Leave It to Beavis

Now that we've established how big government funding problems are likely to be . . . let's think about who will end up bearing most of the costs.

Economist Laurence Kotlikoff of Boston University has developed a type of analysis called "generational accounting" that estimates how much of the burden for government spending is likely to be borne by each successive generation. Using basically the same type of chilling data that leads to uncontrollable debt explosions in the CBO analysis discussed above, he calculated in 1994 that, under then-current policy, future generations would face an 82 percent lifetime net tax rate!

This reminds us of Groucho Marx in *A Night at the Opera.*

After inviting a wealthy society matron to dinner, he was confronted with a large bill that he could not afford. Rising angrily, he handed the bill to the matron, declaring, "This is ridiculous! If I were you, I wouldn't pay it!" He then stomped quickly out of the restaurant.

Kotlikoff's work is another clever way of showing that U.S. fiscal policy is on an unsustainable path. For boomers, it suggests a simple choice: Cope with some combination of higher taxes and lower future benefits beginning soon, or face draconian choices after retiring. For younger generations, it suggests that they face an acceleration of what is now a century-long process of making each successive generation pay more taxes than it receives back in benefits.

Naturally, Kotlikoff's 82 percent net tax rate on future generations will not materialize. That's because our political system is basically designed to produce compromises. If it's a question of cutting retirees' benefits or raising taxes on existing workers, we can expect a little bit of both. If it's a question of whether to tax the wealthy, the middle class, or the poor, the answer is all of the above. If it's a question of making painful choices now or letting our children deal with the problems, we will try to spread the pain.

Of course, the political system is hardly unbiased. As noted earlier, middle-aged and elderly voters tend to have a disproportionate voice in policy decisions because they vote with much greater frequency than the young. So as the baby boomers age, gray power will become an increasingly formidable force at the polls. As aging boomers fight harder to prevent their benefits from being cut, the bills will fall on their children and their children's children.

In short, our political system has a Leave-It-to-Beavis bias that will try to saddle Generation X and younger cohorts with the ballooning costs of caring for the boomers in their retirement years. Accordingly, many analysts have warned of coming generational warfare during the . . . period when painful fiscal adjustments will finally become unavoidable.

Our best guess is that over the next decade the political system will deal with about one third to one half of the entitlements spending problem. Many of those cuts will come through relatively painless measures that will reduce boomers' future entitlements before they are fully aware of what they are losing. . . .

But this scenario still leaves massive adjustments . . . that will urgently need to be tackled during the boomers' retirement years. Such adjustments are likely to be far more painful and politically contentious. By then, all of the low-hanging fruit will have been picked, and politicians will need to propose highly controversial cuts in medical benefits for boomers, or onerous tax hikes for their working children and grandchildren.

Journalist Craig Karpel writes imaginatively of formerly affluent yuppies "picking through dumpsters for cans to sell and scraps to eat." He envisions this group ending up as "dumpies": Destitute Unprepared Mature People. Such scenarios are probably too extreme, because we have seen other modern industrial economies successfully make massive fiscal adjustments of the size needed in the United States. The recent examples of Italy and Sweden come to mind. Their fiscal cutbacks have been extremely painful, but hardly apocalyptic.

That said, the politics of such adjustments are almost certain to be extremely contentious. It is highly predictable that as the boomers age, U.S. politics will become more polarized. Boomer politicians who dedicate themselves to preserving generous entitlements for seniors with inadequate savings should find large audiences. Likewise, young politicians are likely to prosper if they specialize in fending off tax hikes required to fund retired boomers. Fed chairman Alan Greenspan recently warned Congress about the political consequences of failing to address Social Security and Medicare finances. Such consequences, he warns, "are going to be terribly destabilizing to this society, because you're going to force a wrench between the younger people in our society at that time and those who are in the process of retiring."

Baby Boomers as Senior Citizens

Daniel Okrent

The baby boom generation has been one of the most fortunate demographic groups in American history. But as they grow older, boomers will be forced to face new challenges in everything from shrinking retirement benefits to hostility from younger taxpayers who must fund their retirement. As journalist Daniel Okrent writes in the following excerpt, this huge demographic group entering old age will put a severe strain on the social and economic capabilities of the United States.

Were you there, back in the beginning? Were you one of the 76 million children born in the most fertile years in American history? If you weren't, you're probably thinking that you really can't take any more boomer solipsism. You've already suffered through a lifetime of references to Woodstock and the Beach Boys and Vietnam. You've gritted your teeth as you endured the preening, self-congratulatory smugness that leads Ken Dychtwald, a gerontologist who has lately made his living warning about the coming boomer bust, to say, "Boomers feel superior to the younger generations. It wouldn't even occur to boomers not to."

But if you were there, especially if you are part of that front-loaded cadre of boomers born between 1946 and 1957, the last thing you want to hear is that you aren't going to have it your way anymore. After all, as Ralph Whitehead Jr., a public service professor at the University of Massachusetts says, "The baby boom was a self-absorbed generation, a generation that defined itself not through sacrifice as its parents had, but through indulgence."

From "Twilight of the Boomers," by Daniel Okrent, *Time*, June 12, 2000. Copyright © 2000 Time Inc. Reprinted with permission.

When you've been walking on water most of your life—when, since you reached adulthood, America has mostly been at peace, the economy has mostly been strong, and you've been part of a group large enough to call the cultural shots—harsh reality makes for a cold shower.

Did I say reality? In a recent survey conducted by the MacArthur Foundation, American 50-year-olds, when asked how old they thought themselves, ignored the evidence of the hairline, the waistline and the calendar, and said 40.

I have news for you, pals: you're not. (Neither am I. I'm 52, which, when I was a teenager imagining the far, far distant coming of the new millennium, is exactly the horrifying age I figured I'd be.) If you're like the overwhelming majority of boomers, your career has hit a brick wall, you haven't saved enough, your pension is underfunded, your health is deteriorating, even the medical advances that will probably extend your life will, in an especially cruel paradox, probably mean that late life will be meaner and more spartan. You'll have a hard time selling the house that you considered your nest egg (the generation behind just won't have enough buyers). And your neighbors' children, simultaneously burdened with the cost of your aging and victimized by the one thing you'll hold onto—your political power—will boil with resentment. Your own kids may get especially peevish: even today, says Rand Corp. economist James P. Smith, "half the adult children with parents who die over age 70 get zero. Parents are living longer, with more health expenses. The first thing to go . . . is bequests to children."

Need more? There are no movies made for people your age, the music on the radio is dreadful, television programmers behave as if you don't exist. In an astonishing merger of boomer aging with boomer self-involvement, Matsushita Electric has built a prototype smart toilet with built-in microsensors that can run an automatic, daily chemical analysis of the user's urine. Stock-market analysts are growing bullish on companies that build nursing homes or manufacture laxatives.

Coming soon: the Metamucil boom.

Here's looking at you, kid.

The slippage probably began on the turf that the boomers seem to have owned for more than three decades: popular culture. Listened to the radio recently? Do you feel any different than your parents must have felt when they first stood aghast as you fell in love with the Beatles? Of course you do—if you're a boomer, you knew then that your musical taste was superior, and you know it today. What about the movies—weren't you watching The Graduate at the same age that these kids are drooling their brains away over Scream XXVI?

Not having movies to go to, music to listen to or television to watch doesn't exactly rank with famine or pestilence as a besetting syndrome, but it is indicative of the larger phenomenon. You know you're fading when even advertisers of new products don't try to reach you anymore because they no longer care what boomers want, or think or spend their money on (unless it is a solution to pesky erectile dysfunction or your annoying estrogen shortage). Says Cathy De-Thorne, executive vice president of the advertising giant Leo Burnett U.S.A.: "Whining baby boomers are mourning the fact that those rules they understood just don't apply anymore." Maybe we need to attend to the commercial wisdom of Hallmark cards, one company that has no problem marketing across generations. Hallmark simply adjusts the product line to conform to demographic trends. Consequently, says Marita Wesely-Clough, trends expert for the company, it will soon be producing more get-well cards for people with "extended illnesses."

But if pop culture has assumed an alien look, so increasingly has the workplace. In a word, says Chicago-based outplacement specialist John Challenger, "baby boomers are getting squeezed" on the job. "They're filling up the ranks of middle management and fighting each other for the executive-level slots. There are just too many of them."

Not to mention plenty of smart, energetic 33-year-olds who are more than eager to step into the shoes of every smart, not-so-energetic 53-year-old—for less money too, and probably with more appropriate new-economy skills. (The guy in the next office who's still having his secretary print out his e-mail must be planning to win the lottery.) Consequently, says Challenger, boomers who haven't reached, and won't reach, the top "are being squeezed from below as well." It's a squeeze that has brought on a psychic shortness of breath: the 1997 National Study of the Changing Workforce, comparing the attitudes of men and women ages 46 to 51 with a similar cadre studied in 1977, exposed the hollowness and the fear creeping up on the leading-edge boomers: in the original survey more than half felt it highly unlikely they'd soon lose their jobs; in the recent survey barely a quarter felt so comfortable.

Such anguish has grown palpable. FORTUNE magazine's career-advice columnist, Anne Fisher, calls the angst pouring in from her boomer readers "a continuing lament," and there's evidence that it will soon become operatic. From the mailbox of Fisher's website, askannie.com: "I'm learning that being over 40 is not only an obstacle, it's more like a brick wall," writes someone who signs himself "Not Dead Yet." Bob C. thinks "younger bosses see . . . older [workers] as a menace." Edward, the realist, writes, "Many of us over 40 have failed to constantly update our skill sets."

The anecdotal evidence certainly supports data that would have 3 out of 4 experienced workers, even in a full-employment economy, fearing for their jobs. Steve Harrigan, 51, of Austin, Texas, asks a question that virtually any leading-edge boomer can relate to: "Where are we?" When Harrigan is sitting in a restaurant, visiting an office or just walking down the street, he wonders, Why does it always seem he's the oldest person in view?

Want more? As unforgiving as the present has become, our future could be bleaker. It is truly stunning how financially unprepared for retirement boomers are. They don't hold nearly as much stock as their parents do, and according to Richard Hokenson, chief economist of Donaldson, Lufkin & Jenrette, when they were younger—filled, no doubt, with a confident belief in boomer immortality, or at least boomer invulnerability—they saved for retirement much less conscientiously than their Gen X counterparts are doing today. As a result, a full 40% of boomers, and 30% of those nearest to retirement, have less than $10,000 in personal savings. That's more than 30 million people who are no better prepared for retirement than they are for a couple of weeks with the family at Disneyworld.

Pensions? Once upon a time, American businesses funded what was known as defined-benefit plans; they were required to contribute whatever amount would guarantee a specific payout. But corporations like to be able to predict their future liabilities, and the defined-benefit approach has rapidly been replaced by the defined-contribution plan: employer and/or employee contributes X dollars, fund trustees invest it, and investment performance determines the payout. It's great in an up market, but, says Michael F. Carter, a benefits

---

New Designs for Aging Baby Boomers

Manufacturers and designers have catered to the needs of baby boomers since the 1950s. Now that the demographic group is getting older—everything from soda bottles to toilets is being redesigned to accommodate their needs.

At Rix, a trendy Santa Monica, California, restaurant, the management keeps spare bifocals on hand to help aging glitterati read the menu. But in test labs nationwide, generation X industrial designers are taking a more hands-on approach to the prospect of 76 million baby boomers struggling to decipher what to order for dinner. They are donning dark goggles, stuffing cotton in their ears, and tying padding around their joints to give them a feeling for the increasingly creaky life of a generation whose oldest members start to turn 55 this year. "It allows industrial designers who are young to get an idea of what it feels like to be older," says Marc Drucker, a consultant at Arthur D. Little in Cambridge, Massachusetts.

Already, the appliances now emerging from drawing boards boast fatter knobs and bigger print on the control panels. But experts like Drucker predict that, as the massive postwar population ages, it will unleash a design revolution that could remake the nation's visual landscape. Not only is Pepsi research-

specialist with the Hay Group, a worldwide human-resources consultancy, "we're beginning to enter what I call the worry period." Older boomers, he says, are right to wonder "what happens if there's a correction in the stock market and it falls off 20%" without swiftly bouncing back?

From the satirical newspaper the Onion: "Long-awaited baby boomer die-off to begin soon, experts say. Before long, tens of millions of members of this irritating generation will achieve what such boomer icons as Jim Morrison, Janis Joplin, Timothy Leary and John Kennedy already have: death. Before long, we will live in a glorious new world in which no one will ever again have to endure tales of Joan Baez's performance at Woodstock. . . . [T]he ravages of age

---

ing an easier-to-grip bottle, but car doorways are getting wider to accommodate boomers' growing girth. And, after years of cell phones and hand-held digital devices shrinking in size, get ready to watch them swell to ease straining boomer eyes. "For years, there's been this trend toward miniaturization," says Mark Dziersk, chair of the Industrial Designers Society of America. "Now, we'll see that reversed."

But nowhere are boomers' increasingly recalcitrant bodies likely to have more impact than in the American bathroom. At Kohler, the Wisconsin plumbing fixtures giant, the hottest new item is the "comfort-height" toilet—2½ inches higher than the regular model—"so you don't have to squat down as far," according to Chris Lohmann, vice president of fixtures marketing. In fact, so great is the baby boom generation's economic clout that Kohler plans to make "comfort-height" its new standard toilet model. The company will also routinely install grab bars in all its showers and add shelves or "transfer areas" to all its tubs. Not that Kohler's ads will refer to the reason for the change. "You show it as hip and trendy," Lohmann explains, "rather than saying, 'It's because you're old'."

Marci McDonald, "New Designs for Aging Hipsters," *U.S. News & World Report*, April 2, 2001.

will take its toll on boomer self-indulgence, and the curtain will at long last fall on what is regarded by many as the most odious generation America has ever produced."

Like all good satire, this hurts because it is, in its essence, so accurate. Where once my generation was celebrated for its commitment to peace and justice, what we've grown to be—what we always were, probably—is a generation committed to nothing more (or less) substantial than what we appear to be leaving as our signal legacy to American culture: casual Fridays.

As you read this sentence, another baby boomer is turning 50. In eight seconds, so will another, and then another, and on and on will this cascade of calendar-enforced maturity continue for the next decade and a half, an entire generation hitting the back nine and turning the world over to those who are younger, faster, fitter, more ambitious. (Even the most commonly used number—the 76 million born in the boom—is a gross underestimate: add 8 million immigrant boomers to the total.) For the present purposes, though, we're going to focus on the leading edge of the boom, those people born between 1946 and 1957 who made it to their teens before the '60s ended. We know self-indulgence better than our younger siblings do, so we're going to feel what's happening next that much more sharply. And, of course, sooner—like, tomorrow.

Evidence? We may claim to feel as if we're 40, but if you really want to know what we've got on our minds, wander the Web to gauge the current state of boomer consciousness. A recently launched site targeted at people over 50, GenerationA.com, boasts of its large-size type fonts. Elsewhere, the author of a regular boomer column begins, "I had some serious dental work done this week." The longest threads in the community section of "Boomer Board" are about estrogen-replacement therapies. A new boomer site, myprimetime.com, has so brazenly donned the generation's narcissistic garment that without irony, it calls its series of cheesy self-evaluation quizzes "Me Meters." On "Are You a Candidate for Burnout?" I scored an 86.

The Marriott chain has opened about 150 managed-retirement communities under the names Brighton Gardens and MapleRidge, apparently confident that boomers will be filling the apartments in 10 years, the assisted-care quarters in 20, the intensive-care units in 30. About 25% of those latter spaces are being specifically reserved for residents with cognitive disorders. Makes sense: while only 8% of people over 65 suffer from the severe memory loss that characterizes Alzheimer's disease, the number leaps to a range of 30% to 47% for those over 85, and we all know that we're going to live longer than our parents. Boomer watcher Dychtwald, in his list of 10 physical, social, spiritual, economic and political crises just ahead, puts "mass dementia" at No. 2.

If you want a glimpse of the boomer future that you'll never see in the ads for Brighton Gardens or MapleRidge (knowingly ironic boomer question: Where do they come up with these names?), travel instead to Rochester, Minn., and the Mayo Clinic. In Dr. Darryl Chutka's classroom, the 10 first-year medical students look a little different from what you might expect. They're all wearing goggles coated in a clear film, ear plugs, heavy rubber gloves, extra-thick socks. They also have marshmallows stuffed in their mouths, corn kernels scattered inside their shoes, stiff, confining braces around their necks—and enormous, padded diapers stuffed inside their underclothes.

What Professor Chutka calls the "Aging Game" is a novel, if slightly frightening, effort to familiarize future physicians with the circumstances of the patients they will be treating when they emerge from their medical training. The goggles simulate cataracts; the ear plugs, loss of hearing; the gloves, arthritis; the socks, edema; the marshmallows, post-stroke paralysis; the corn, bunions; the neck braces, the nearly universal muscular stiffness of old age. The diapers . . . well, the diapers are indicative of what managers at Kimberly-Clark consider the promising future of the market for "adult-incontinence products," one of their fastest-growing areas of business.

Wearing all this stuff is the easy part of the aging game; what's harder is performing the various tasks Chutka demands of the students, like reading the labels on a vast array of prescription containers when you're wearing goggles, or counting out the daily ration of pills with fingers rendered numb by a sheath of glove rubber. Near the course's end, the students are placed in a mock nursing home, where other students, trained to act like ward attendants, fail to bring them their food, or shove spoonfuls of apple sauce into mouths rendered immobile by the marshmallows or ignore them altogether. "They wheeled me into a corner, and it was so hard to see and hear anything," remembers third-year student Melissa Niesen. "It was really depressing."

Useful, though: "It's definitely in the minds of my classmates," Niesen adds, "that we will be seeing a lot more older individuals in our practices."

That's you, Mr. and Mrs. Boomer. The good news is that you will be retiring younger than your parents and living longer than them too; in fact, if you started your career at 23, are one of the few sufficiently well off to be able to retire at 55, and live to be 90, you will spend more than half your adulthood in retirement—an unprecedented reconfiguration of life's traditional arc. But in what physical condition will you spend those years? And with what financial resources will you be able to finance them?

The best case would see the entire Sun Belt populated by a new cadre of semi-retirees, fit and healthy, working part time from their homes while enjoying the fruits of well-invested savings and well-funded pension plans. That's what the management is counting on at the headquarters of the Del Webb Corp. in Phoenix, Ariz., developers of the Sun City chain of retirement communities. Del Webb executives are quivering in anticipation of a flood of boomers pouring into the retirement-home market. LeRoy Hanneman, 54, Del Webb's CEO, stands on a hill from which he can see his company's future as vividly as he can mix metaphors: "The explosion of baby boomers is like a freight train bearing down on us," he says. "Del Webb has already laid the tracks for the future, and we expect to benefit mightily."

Before he adds a single unit to the nearly 72,460 Sun City houses his company has built in the past 40 years, Hanneman is investing $100 million to $150 million in research to understand the needs and wants of what research director Paul Bessler calls the "new bodies" moving into his company's focus. "The opportunity is just incredible for us," Bessler says, to provide homes for those few fortunate enough and farsighted enough to have developed sufficient skills, harbored appropriate attitudes and, probably most important, put away enough money for a retirement that is going to take on a shape we've never seen before. Based on its research, Del Webb already outfits its new houses with high-capacity wiring for home offices and offers options such as home exercise rooms. Integrated computer, security and entertainment systems will be the next must-haves in boomer retirement housing.

In fact, the Del Webb version of the future sounds pretty nice, the kind of fantasy that most of us have imagined at one time or another, and that, if everything breaks exactly right, a few of us will certainly experience: fit, healthy and well off, we will enjoy all those things—exotic travel, continuing education, 36 holes a day—that we could neither afford nor find the time for while we were raising our families. Professionally, we'll be called upon as part-time consultants by younger workers eager for the wisdom born of experience, or we will generously donate our time and skills to our favorite causes. Our children and grandchildren, so pleased with how well Mom and Pop are doing, will visit often, each time drinking thirstily from the vessels of kindly wisdom that we have miraculously become.

But even if we're living the high life in Maple Boomer Retirement Ridge Heaven, don't expect us to mellow much, to lessen our demands, our insistent wish that the world pay attention to us, us, us!!! In a Del Webb survey of boomer attitudes, respondents said their greatest contribution in retirement will include "demanding funding for medical research." The red ribbon for AIDS and the pink ribbon of breast cancer will be replaced by gray ribbons of gerontology.

And so, inevitably, will the funds to combat those diseases be channeled elsewhere. For the Del Webb interviewees also expected to be "setting the political agenda," and these four words may be even more important to the American future than the expected medical advances. There are today 3.4 wage-earning (and Social Security–contributing) American workers for every person over 65. In 2030 there will be only two workers for each of the elderly (which is why economist Hokenson, of DLJ, calls Social Security "the mother of all Ponzi schemes"). Those two are either going to have to work a lot harder to support all the old folks, or we will see a spectacle of misery unprecedented in the world's wealthiest nation. Two irrefutable facts, the size of the boomer generation and the tendency of the elderly to vote in greater percentages than any other age group, will converge to create a daunting political force.

And with it, a strong chance of intergenerational conflict. "Watch for tension to increase among generations as the boomers enter their late 50s," says Dr. David Reuben, who heads the geriatrics division at the UCLA School of Medicine. Noting that "it costs between $35,000 and $50,000 a year [to support] one person in a nursing facility," a strapped nation will, Reuben concludes, have to choose between caring for its children or its parents. Have you ever noticed how the elderly in your town vote when a proposal to raise property taxes to pay for education hits the local ballot? Count on it: this time, through the scrupulous, if self-interested, exercise of their franchise, boomers will yank the reins of society out of the hands of their children. In every other sphere, we may be every bit as faded as a poster from the original Woodstock. But here, in one final effort to forestall Boomerdammerung, we will summon the vigor to plant our solipsistic flagpole, piercing the heart of the larger society.

Thus casual Friday may not be our final legacy after all. Instead, we may create a gerontocracy of such unity and might that it will either utterly dominate the American political map or provoke all-out generational warfare. In a nation in which only 66 million vote in off-year congressional elections, a bloc of some 80 million people motivated by their desperate self-interest will become dauntingly powerful.

Now be honest, fellow children of the boom: Is this good news or bad?

Appendix of Documents

Document 1: The First Rock and Roll Movies

The first rock and roll many baby boomers ever heard was Bill Haley's "Rock Around the Clock," which jolted audiences at the beginning of the 1955 movie The Blackboard Jungle. *As rock journalist Ed Ward explains, other fifties movies about juvenile delinquents inspired many teenagers to act out antisocial behavior glamorized on the silver screen.*

Life had reported on a new movie, *The Blackboard Jungle*, based on a novel by Evan Hunter, in which a new teacher at a high school in a "bad" section of town is taunted and abused by a group of his students (including a black one, portrayed by Sidney Poitier). Among the terrible things they do to one of his fellow teachers is mock his taste in music when he tries to reach them through playing some jazz records in class. They laugh and throw the priceless discs around the classroom as the teacher stands frozen with fright, watching his collection being smashed to bits. This disgusting bit of behavior was not lost on a lot of the teenagers who flocked to see *The Blackboard Jungle*. When the theme song, Bill Haley's not-too-successful record of 1954, "Rock Around the Clock," came on at the start of the movie, they'd dance on the seats, which were frequently not up to the chore and collapsed. Then the teenagers would throw the broken seats at each other.

This movie and others addressed to the insatiable teenage audience fed public fears of "juvenile delinquency," the disease that had teens committing senseless crimes, indulging in alcohol and cigarettes and premarital sex, riding motorcycles or driving hopped-up cars, and listening to rock and roll. First there had been *The Wild One* in 1953, in which Marlon Brando and a gang of thugs on motorcycles terrorized a town, something that had really happened in the mountains above San Bernardino, California, where a group of war veterans who had formed a motorcycle club named after a war movie, *Hell's Angels*, had just taken over for a weekend. At least the *Blackboard Jungle* kids were from the slums, so there was an excuse for their behavior. But the 1955 *Rebel Without a Cause*, based on a real case history from California psychiatrist Robert Lindner, featured teen idol James Dean sympathetically portraying a screwed-up kid who just didn't seem to care, no matter how his parents tried to steer him right. The film blasphemously seemed to be placing the blame for Dean's antisocial behavior on his parents and on society at large! It was a stretched-out exposition of Marlon Brando's famed line in *The Wild One*, when he is asked what he's rebelling against. "Whaddya got?" he replies. And teens were eating up these movies, seeing them literally dozens of times. It did no good to explain to parents that teenagers like Brando and Dean were a distinct minority, or, as President Eisenhower once put it, that "teenagers are like airplanes: You only hear about the ones that crash."

And in May 1955, it was discovered that class distinctions had nothing to do with rock and roll's ability to incite the baser passions: at Princeton University, it was reported, a student fired up "Rock Around the Clock" in his dorm room, and was answered right afterward by another student doing the same thing. Soon a mob had formed in the courtyard, chanting and stamping their feet, setting fire to trash cans as they moved beyond the halls of Old Nassau into the streets at midnight, until finally a dean was found to quell the boiling blue blood, reminding them of the dire consequences of being thrown out of Princeton.

Rock of Ages: The Rolling Stone *History of Rock & Roll*. New York: Rolling Stone Press, 1986.

Document 2: Irreverent Reading Material

Although the fifties typically are portrayed as an era of dull conformity, Mad *magazine was one subversive element that was widely read by teenagers during that time. As social critics Jane and Michael Stern write, the irreverent and hilarious* Mad *ridiculed nearly everything that Americans held sacred.*

What rock and roll did for the bodies of the baby boom, *Mad* magazine did for our minds. It was cultural liberation in the form of parody, and for many who grew up reading it, *Mad* was every bit as titillating and taboo as *Playboy* or Elvis Presley's dancing pelvis. It was a monthly dose of blasphemy and disrespect that was the polar opposite of the Walt Disney pieties well-behaved children were supposed to be ingurgitating. And make no mistake, it was kids who composed most of the *Mad* readership: kids who were beginning to feel rebellious; not yet empowered, but on their way to creating a serious generation gap. "If you were growing up lonely and isolated in a small town, *Mad* was a revelation," recalled "Head Comix" artist R. Crumb. "Nothing I read anywhere else suggested there was any absurdity in the culture. *Mad* was like a shock, breaking you out."

It began publication in 1952, looking like a horror comic book, with a cover that advertised "Tales Calculated to Drive You MAD" and the subtitle "Humor in a Jugular Vein." It contained four features, each a parody of a comic book. The cover showed a couple cowering in the dungeon.

"That thing, that slithering blob coming towards us!" screams the man.

"What is it?" screams the woman.

And piping up from the ground, a finger digging deep into one nostril, their gnome-like child delivers the answer: "It's Melvin!"

Of such wisenheimer non sequiturs and deflated expectations was *Mad* made. Eventually, each issue contained well over a dozen different features: essays, comic-book and TV and movie parodies, sheet-music spoofs, fold-ins (as opposed to *Playboy*'s expanding centerfold), articles pretending to advise readers how to improve their lives. Nothing was ever serious, and nothing was sacred. *Mad* ripped into almost every respected institution and accepted wisdom, into fringe groups and conformists, into trendy lifestyles (from 1950s suburban to 1980s yuppie), into politics (the John Birch Society, the Ku Klux Klan, black militants, the New Left, the Kennedys, Nixon, Bush), into psychoanalysis and the New Age human potential movement, into Shakespeare as well as the lowest-brow pop culture, into Barbie dolls and bikers. . . .

Early issues of *Mad* made fun of Christmas, Superman and Wonder Woman, Mickey Mouse, Howdy Doody, Picasso paintings, the Gettysburg Address, comic books and—most deliciously—advertisements for all the products that billed themselves as essential to a happy life in these United States. Cigarettes, cars, barbecue grills, and fashionable clothing were all rendered stupid-looking by *Mad*'s ad parodies; and even the most juvenile readers couldn't help looking at such ridicule and begin to cultivate their own countercultural point of view. *Mad* presented itself as an antidote to sanctimony with only one consistent principle: to give the raspberry to all the overly anointed aspects of American life. . . .

Nowadays, *Mad* has plenty of company in its impolite crusade, but in the 1950s and early 1960s it was alone. By wrapping its derision in juvenile buffoonery, it helped ensconce subversion as a fundamental attitude of postwar adolescence.

Encyclopedia of Pop Culture. New York: HarperPerennial, 1987.

Document 3: The Beatniks' Influence on Hippies

The counterculture movement of the 1960s was greatly influenced by poets, painters, and writers of the fifties beatnik era, as art and social critic Thomas Albright explains in the April 27, 1968, issue of Rolling Stone.

The Beats formed the first large-scale, self-conscious and widely publicized group of middle-class dropouts—this, at a time when the standard transition was from Boy Scout uniform to army khaki to gray flannel [business] suit. The Establishment was appropriately enraged, and the Beats were understandably agonized and torn within themselves. . . .

For the most part, the Beats functioned within the Establishment—hung out in Establishment bars, donned suits to pick up unemployment checks or work in Establishment jobs; no other facilities existed, the Beats were relatively few in number and isolation was a key fact of existence. There was a greater sense of community than the Beats are generally now given credit for but organization was anathema, and such community as there was was informal, an encounter and then a drawing apart, activism centered on such spur-of-the-moment issues as raising bail for someone the cops had hauled away.

At the same time, the Beats were, psychologically, much more intensely . . . alienated from the Establishment than are the hippies, with all their subculture; such relations as were necessary— paying a cover charge, perhaps working—were accepted with the irony accorded such facts of life as going to the john. But there was no move at all toward a rapprochement (except to put on an inquiring journalist) and, especially in the area of art, any success with the Establishment was scornfully regarded as a sell-out. The Beats dislodged their cultural roots by reveling in urban rootlessness with its outcast subcultures. The hippies, a truly rootless generation, seek roots in nature, in the cult of the American Indian, in the ancient traditions of Oriental thought.

Sociologically, and psychologically, the main contrasts between the Beat and the hippie eras are in terms of isolation vs. community, opposition vs. separate-but-equal relationship to the Establishment, social apathy vs. activism and pessimism vs. optimism. No one can begin to explain these changes in terms of particular causes, but part of the reason certainly lies in the difference of sheer numbers—the coming of age of the postwar baby boom— and in a group consciousness fostered in the first generation to be reared in front of a television set. There was the fact of Kennedy, who galvanized the entire nation from apathy to activism—between the Beat and hippie periods came the brief but important era of the Berkeley militants and the folk revival—and there is an optimism that survived the assassination. . . .

And there has been a parallel change in the Establishment itself—shaken by a series of crises, from Korea and the Beats to civil rights and Vietnam. Over the years, the walls have cracked to admit many of the rebels of the Fifties—jazz fans, appreciators of abstract expressionism, pot-smokers, a number of the Beats themselves, sometimes in such influential roles as college professors. And the thing that the Beats had started captured the imagination of successive waves of self-aware and disenchanted youth, who in succeeding years developed and modified the lifestyle into the hippie community of today.

Holly George-Warren, ed., *The Rolling Stone Book of the Beats.* New York: Hyperion, 1999.

Document 4: Reactions to Kennedy's Assassination

The assassination of President John F. Kennedy in Dallas in 1963 shattered the childhood innocence of many baby boomers and ushered in a decade of social chaos. Ever after, almost everyone alive on that day remembered exactly what they were doing when they heard the tragic news. In the following excerpt, historian and author Tom Shachtman gives a historical snapshot of that riveting day in November.

During the lunch hour in Dallas on November 22, 1963, while he was riding through the downtown streets in an open limousine and smiling and waving to sidewalk crowds, President John F. Kennedy was assassinated.

Apart from the detonation of the atomic bomb at Hiroshima, the murder of President Kennedy was the single most shocking event of our time. Reverberations from the act are still being felt today. The assassination shattered the time of complacency that had existed in the United States since the close of World War II and ushered in an era of uncertainty and anguish.

Kennedy's position, age, and personality added to the shock of the assassination. Young, smiling, popular, the president embodied a great spirit, an eagerness for the use of power that was tempered by vision and purpose. Though many disagreed with his policies and methods, there were few who disparaged his engaging personality or who wished him bodily harm. There was every expectation that the remainder of his term would be filled with progressive ideas, and that he would win a second term in 1964.

The reaction of the country to Kennedy's death was nearly as instantaneous and as explosive as the rifle shots themselves. This was a moment of intense emotion, a public and private tragedy. . . . Bad news traveled fast: according to a study made by the National Opinion Research Center, before the end of the afternoon 99.8 percent of the population knew that the president was dead. Half learned by word of mouth; then for verification most turned to the electronic media.

Americans shared a tremendous sense of loss. From the time of the assassination on Friday until mid-Monday when the slain president was laid to rest, the three television networks broadcast without commercial interruption every detail of the event and its aftermath. This was the greatest simultaneous event in the history of the world, and it bequeathed to us a series of indelible images. We watched television ten hours a day and saw: the assassination site from every angle; the unloading of the casket from *Air Force One* in the rain; Lyndon Johnson's agonized face and his plea for our help and God's; the murder of Lee Harvey Oswald by Jack Ruby; the stream of high-level mourners in the East Room of the White House; dignitaries and heads of state of ninety-two nations come to pay homage; the stoic honor guard; the funeral cortege with its riderless horse and reversed boots in the stirrups; little John-John [Kennedy's] salute; Mrs. Kennedy's remarkable fortitude; the grave and the eternal flame in Arlington National Cemetery.

Tom Shachtman, *Decade of Shocks: Dallas to Watergate, 1963–1974.* New York: Poseidon Press, 1983.

Document 5: Race Riots and Vietnam

During the turbulent 1960s, hundreds of riots erupted in inner-city black neighborhoods across the country. In the Watts neighborhood of Los Angeles, buildings burned, people were shot, and fully armed National Guardsmen patrolled the streets in jeeps and tanks. Some inner-city residents could see little difference between their situation and the war in Vietnam. Eldridge Cleaver eloquently put these feelings into words and became a hero to both black and white activists in the New Left movement.

A strange thing happened in Watts, in 1965, August. The blacks, who in this land of private property have all private and no property, got excited into an uproar because they noticed a cop before he had a chance to wash the blood off his hands. Usually the police department can handle such flare-ups. But this time it was different. Things got out of hand. The blacks were running amok, burning, shooting, breaking. The police department was powerless to control them; the chief called for reinforcements. Out came the National Guard, that ambiguous hybrid from the twilight zone where the domestic army merges with the international; that hypocritical force poised within America and capable of action on either level, capable of backing up either the police or the armed forces. Unleashing their formidable firepower, they crushed the blacks. But things will never be the same again. Too many people saw that those who turned the other cheek in Watts got their whole head blown off. At the same time, heads were being blown off in Vietnam. America was embarrassed, not by the quality of her deeds but by the surplus of publicity focused upon her negative selling points, and a little frightened because of what all those dead bodies, on two fronts, implied. Those corpses spoke eloquently of potential allies and alliances. A community of interest began to emerge, dripping with blood, out of the ashes of Watts. The blacks in Watts and all over America could now see the Viet Cong's point: both were on the receiving end of what the armed forces were dishing out.

Eldridge Cleaver, *Soul on Ice*. New York: Dell, 1968.

Document 6: The Influence of the Beatles

The Beatles were the premier rock band of the 1960s, and their influence changed everything from hair styles to the way music was recorded in a studio. John Parikhal, a baby boomer business expert, describes the influence of the groundbreaking Beatles album Sgt. Pepper's Lonely Hearts Club Band *on his generation.*

Strangely enough, I first heard *Sgt. Pepper* on AM radio in Miami. By the time the album was released, the Beatles were such big news that many radio stations sent disc jockeys to England to pick up a copy of the album before it was released in the United States. They premiered it with enormous fanfare, capitalizing on the fact that the Beatles were larger than life.

Even on an AM radio station, the music was radically different, revolutionary, and creatively exceptional. I couldn't wait to buy the album. When I bought *Sgt. Pepper* a week later, another surprise lay in store for me. It included a lyric sheet! This was wonderful. Instead of having to listen to a song fifteen or twenty times to figure out the lyrics, I could get into it right away. It was poetry and music combined.

Sgt. Pepper was the culmination of the Beatles' experimentation with drugs, religion, technological recording techniques, and their own growth toward adulthood. It was so different from anything that had happened in rock music before that it challenged listeners to expand themselves when they listened to the music. One of the most popular ways to do this was to experiment with marijuana or psychedelic drugs such as mescaline and LSD.

Sgt. Pepper completed the transformation of our generation from clean-cut, obedient kids to experimenters who seriously questioned the status quo. And it all happened so fast.

In 1964, hardly anyone had long hair, marijuana was a "bad" drug associated with Beatniks, and no one in their right mind would want to induce schizophrenia chemically. Just over four years later, long hair was the new status quo, drug experimentation was spreading faster than a brush fire, and parents everywhere were confronted by strangers they used to call their children.

Although *Sgt. Pepper* didn't cause the change, it provided the necessary symbol to our generation. It said that experimentation could produce greatness, that music was the handmaiden of growth, and that we were entering a new world for which we had never been prepared.

John Parikhal, *The Baby Boom: Making Sense of Our Generation at Forty.* Ontario, Canada: Joint Communications Corporation, 1993.

Document 7: The Birth of Gay Liberation

The modern gay liberation movement is widely said to have begun on Friday evening, June 27, 1969, when the New York City police raided the Stonewall Inn, a popular Greenwich Village gay bar. Although patrons of gay bars were routinely harassed by police for minor infractions, this time the crowd spilled out onto the street and began to fight back. For the next several nights protests and arrests ensued. Dubbed the Stonewall Riots, this small resistance propelled the gay rights movement onto the front pages of newspapers and magazines. In the following years, gay rights would become an important issue across the country. But as journalist Lucian Truscott IV wrote in the July 3, 1969, Village Voice, *the early protests divided the more flamboyant baby boom gays from older homosexuals who disliked the media attention the movement was attracting.*

Cops entered the Stonewall for the second time in a week just before midnight on Friday. It began as a small raid—only two patrolmen, two detectives, and two policewomen were involved. But as the patrons trapped inside were released one by one, a crowd started to gather on the street. It was initially a festive gathering, composed mostly of Stonewall boys who were waiting around for friends still inside or to see what was going to happen. Cheers would go up as favorites would emerge from the door, strike a pose, and swish by the detective with a "Hello there, fella." The stars were in their element. Wrists were limp, hair was primped, and reactions to the applause were classic. "I gave them the gay power bit, and they loved it, girls." "Have you seen Maxine? Where *is* my wife—I told her not to go far."

Suddenly the paddywagon arrived and the mood of the crowd changed. Three of the more blatant queens—in full drag—were loaded inside, along with the bartender and doorman, to a chorus of catcalls and boos from the crowd. A cry went up to push the paddywagon over, but it drove away before anything could happen. With its exit, the action waned momentarily. The next person to come out was a dyke, and she put up a struggle—from car to door to car again. It was at that moment that the scene became explosive. Limp wrists were forgotten. Beer cans and bottles were heaved at the windows, and a rain of coins descended on the cops. At the height of the action a bearded figure was plucked from the crowd and dragged inside. It was [folksinger] Dave Van Ronk, who had come from the Lion's Head to see what was going on. He was later charged with having thrown an object at the police.

Three cops were necessary to get Van Ronk away from the crowd and into the Stonewall. The exit left no cops on the street, and almost by signal the crowd erupted into cobblestone and bottle heaving. The reaction was total; they were pissed. The trash can I was standing on was nearly yanked out from under me as a kid tried to grab it for use in the window-smashing melee. From nowhere came an uprooted parking meter—used as a battering ram on the Stonewall door. I heard several cries of "Let's get some gas," but the blaze of flame which soon appeared in the window of the Stonewall was still a shock. As the wood barrier behind the glass was beaten open, the cops inside turned their hose on the crowd. Several kids took the opportunity to cavort in the spray, and their momentary glee served to stave off what was rapidly becoming a full-scale attack. By the time the fags were able to regroup forces and come up with another assault, several carloads of police reinforcements had arrived, and in minutes the streets were clear.

A visit to the Sixth Precinct revealed that thirteen persons had been arrested on charges that ranged from Van Ronk's felonious assault of a police officer to the owners' illegal sale and storage of alcoholic beverages without a license. Two police officers had been injured in the battle with the crowd. By the time the last cop was off the street Saturday morning, a sign was going up that the Stonewall would reopen that night. It did.

Protest set the tone for the "gay power" activities on Saturday. The afternoon was spent boarding up the windows of the Stonewall and chalking them with signs of the new revolution: "We are open," "There is all college boys and girls in here," "Support Gay Power— C'mon in girls." "[Police inspector] Smyth looted our money, juke-box, cigarette mach., telephones, safe, cash register, and the boys' tips." Among the slogans were two carefully clipped and bordered copies of the *Daily News* story about the previous night's events, which was anything but kind to the gay cause.

The real action Saturday was that night on the street. Friday night's crowd had returned and was being led in "gay power" cheers by a group of gay cheerleaders. "We are the Stonewall girls/We wear our hair in curls/We have no underwear/We show our pubic hairs!" The crowd was gathered across the street from the Stonewall and was growing with additions of onlookers, East-siders, and rough street people who saw a chance for a little action. Though dress had changed from Friday night's gayery to Saturday night street clothes, the scene was a command performance for queers. If Friday night had been pick-up night, Saturday was date night. Hand-holding, kissing, and posing accented each of the cheers with a homosexual liberation that had appeared only fleet-ingly on the street before. One-liners were as practiced as if they had been used for years. "I just want you to all know," quipped a platinum blond with obvious glee, "that sometimes being a homo-sexual is a big pain in the ass." Another allowed as how he had be-come a "left-deviationist." And on and on.

The quasi-political tone of the street scene was looked upon with disdain by some, for radio news announcements about the previous night's "gay power" chaos had brought half of Fire Is-land's Cherry Grove* running back to home base to see what they had left behind. The generation gap existed even here. Older boys had strained looks on their faces and talked in concerned whispers as they watched the up-and-coming generation take being gay and flaunting it before the masses.

*Fire Island, on the south shore of Long Island, was a major summer beach resort for New York. It had several gay communities, including Cherry Grove—ed.

Excerpted from "Gay Power Comes to Sheridan Square," Lucian Truscott IV, *The Village Voice*, July 3, 1969. Reprinted by permission of the author.

Document 8: Empowered by Women's Liberation

After a decade of protesting the war in Vietnam and striking for civil rights, women began to demand their own equal protection under the law. Gloria Steinem, political activist and cofounder of Ms. *magazine, covered some early events as a reporter, and recalls the obstacles women faced in a society not ready to abandon institutional sexism.*

In February [1969], the New York state legislature in Albany held hearings on abortion—this was before the liberalization of the law—and fourteen men and one nun were invited to testify. A group of feminists decided that made no sense at all, and soon after, decided to hold their own hearings in a church basement downtown in [Greenwich] Village. I had a regular political column then for *New York* magazine, and so went down to cover their hearings. . . .

When I listened to those women at the hearing, I knew something very deep had started to change in them—and in me. It was one of the most incredible meetings I've ever seen. Women stood up and told the truth about their lives. They weren't talking about statistics, or [the Vietnam] war thousands of miles away, or fighting imperialism from the top down. They were telling the truth about what it was like to have an abortion.

You could see that most of the women had never talked about this in public before. Same of the stories were tragic, some were funny. Most of them were about risky and humiliating experiences. One very shy young woman wearing a dress with a white collar got up. She said that she had been pregnant when she was seventeen or eighteen. Her parents were poor, and she hadn't known where to go for help. She went to hospitals and was made to stand up before examining boards and explain how she'd gotten pregnant, where she'd been, how many times she'd had intercourse. At least one hospital agreed to perform an abortion only if she would be sterilized.

Other women talked about entering the criminal underground to find an abortionist—the shame of it, and the danger. One woman told us that her boyfriend had convinced her that she couldn't get pregnant after the second or third orgasm. The audience broke up in laughter. It was like the early civil rights meetings; women were moved to stand up and testify. They were telling the truth about something they had been forced to conceal all their lives.

I'd also had an abortion. I had never told anyone except the doctor. Not a friend, not the man involved. No one. I didn't stand up and say it at the meeting, but afterward, I felt free to talk about it for the first time. I began to read more feminist literature; it made sense to me intellectually *and* emotionally. My other political understandings seemed intellectual and learned, but this was organic. The column I wrote for *New York* magazine was called "After Black Power, Women's Liberation?" I was too insecure to use a period, so I used a question mark. . . .

The article in *New York* was my "coming out" as a feminist. Male journalists who had been my friends for years took me aside very kindly and said, "Look, you've worked very hard to be taken seriously as a journalist. If you identify yourself with all these crazy feminists, you'll ruin yourself." When I kept at it, they encouraged antifeminist women in *New York* to write counterarticles.

The next year, the piece that my male colleagues hated so much won a journalism prize as a first above-ground report on this wave of feminism, on women's liberation. But still they took me aside and told me that I'd destroy myself, and that I could never be taken seriously again. After all, it was a prize for writing on women, so it didn't count.

I wanted to write about women in a new, serious, political way—and nobody was interested. Either they said I was a woman and couldn't be objective, or they said, "We published our feminist article last year." After a few months, I gave up and started to lecture.

This in itself was revolutionary for me. I was very nervous. I had a major terror of public speaking and yet I cared so much about explaining what feminism really was (as opposed to bra-burning, as the press was saying) that I forced myself to speak. I spoke in tandem with black feminist friends—first Dorothy Pitman Hughes, then Flo Kennedy or Margaret Sloan. We did this consciously in order to say that feminism meant *all* women, not just the integration of a few privileged women into patriarchal systems.

We were often ridiculed. Men would come up with a big smile and say, "I'm a male chauvinist." A man stopped me in the street and said, "I have ten women employees and I pay them a third of what I pay men, and if I had to pay them more, I'd fire them. What do you think of *that?*" It was as if they could get rid of the whole contagious idea by getting rid of a few troublemakers. . . .

I've often found myself in a . . . can't-win dilemma. If you are conventionally attractive, you do well in the world; people say that you got there through men. If you're not pretty, they say that you're doing it because you couldn't get a man. If you really stand up for yourself and for other women, they say you're a lesbian. That's the worst dilemma—lesbians are twice discriminated against, so you feel disloyal if you are not a lesbian. Should you tell the truth about your private life?

The best retort I ever heard was at a feminist lecture down South. A hostile man stood up in the back and directed the question at Flo. "Are you a lesbian?" She said, "Are you my alternative?" He sat back down.

Lynda Rosen Obst, ed., *The Sixties: The Decade Remembered Now by the People Who Lived Then.* New York: Rolling Stone Press, 1977.

Document 9: New Attitudes Toward Food

Although baby boomers were only the first generation reared on processed, additive-laden food and TV dinners, some began to question the wholesomeness of these provisions as they established families of their own. As author Arthur Stein writes, sixties political activism gave rise to the co-op food market and the modern health food movement.

By the late 1960s increasing societal ferment again led more Americans to seek out . . . or create alternative economic institutions. Continuing through the 1970s there was a marked increase in consumer cooperatives, often located in small storefronts or basements, or in people's homes. They sprouted up in and around universities and also in local neighborhoods.

There are many forms of cooperative ventures, concerned with food production and distribution, transportation, housing, child care, and other activities. I will note here the most widely known and experienced form in the 1970s and 1980s—the consumer food co-op. . . .

According to the authors of the useful *Food Co-op Handbook*, cooperatives could be defined as "non-profit, democratically controlled groups of consumers that distribute high quality food, try to educate themselves . . . and seek to represent an alternative to the mainstream profit-oriented food industry.". . .

In general people start co-ops for one or more of these reasons: (1) to obtain better-quality products or services more cheaply; (2) to provide an alternative to existing product/service delivery systems and institutions, in other words, supermarkets; (3) to demonstrate that radical, new, or different ideas can work—for example, consensual decision making; and (4) to promote a cooperative way of life. The goals of the Alternative, as rearticulated in a co-op manual in 1981, are "to become involved in the process of providing whole foods (with as little packaging and processing as possible) at low prices—as an alternative to mass-processed foods of limited nutritional value. Members run the co-op, buying directly from wholesalers and local producers and providing all the necessary labor to keep the store well-stocked and operating smoothly."

As a nonprofit co-op the Alternative provides members with a wide variety of quality goods, cooking utensils, and the like. Whenever possible it acquires foodstuffs that are grown organically (without chemicals or pesticides). Food prices are kept down because the overhead is low. Members stock the shelves, record the prices, and bring their own bags and jars to carry home the unprocessed foods they buy in bulk. They do the purchasing and inventory and clean up the molasses or flour that may have spilled on the floor.

The experiences of working voluntarily together and sharing responsibilities are valuable in themselves. The skills necessary to organize and operate a co-op and build cooperative interpersonal relations are transferable to other aspects of our lives in a society that often lacks opportunities to develop such abilities. . . .

The co-op is also a place where people can come together in a pleasant environment that they have created. It offers an appropriate setting for community-based activities and serves as an information exchange for social and political activities in the surrounding communities. Parents don't have to worry about their children grabbing candy at the checkout counter, and a children's play area is provided. . . .

The co-op focuses on consumer self-education—there is no commercial need to influence customers to buy products or to disguise ingredients or true price. Information is available on the sources and nutritional value of all products sold. The possibility of theft is also minimal; it would be like stealing from one's friends. Classes are offered on wok cookery, tofu making, tai chi, yoga, weaving, and alternative health care. The co-op is a place to pass out those extra zucchini grown in the home garden, distribute flower bulbs and cutting, and share recipes. Members can have the pleasure of grinding fresh, warm flour in the grain mill an hour before baking bread at home. . . .

Alternative members take surplus food to a nearby home for the elderly, where they can discuss nutrition and health and swap stories with the residents. Members can also undertake a variety of other educational and creative outreach activities.

Arthur Stein, *Seeds of the Seventies.* Hanover, NH: University Press of New England, 1985.

Document 10: Growing Up and Changing Values

By the 1980s, many former hippies had become status-conscious yuppies, sometimes hard-pressed to explain this stunning reversal of roles. In the following excerpt, Harvard business professor D. Quinn Mills relates a conversation between a real couple named Susan and Bif, who discuss their personal transformations over the years.

"Do you remember that summer we spent in New Mexico?" Susan asked.

"Yes," Bif responded, his expression quizzical.

"I like to think back to those days," Susan continued. "When I met you, I was being a hippie. I had long straight hair and love beads. I wore white lipstick and huge gold earrings in my ears. I had thick black eyeliner on my eyes that came up to a point. I used to just tie a scarf around my chest instead of wearing a blouse or a shirt. I was probably dressed like that when we met.

"I remember when I was a senior in high school, I would go out to the school bus and all the girls would gather at the back of the bus. We'd all kind of squeeze together so the boys couldn't see and we'd slip out of our bras. You couldn't wear a bra in those days, but you wouldn't dare go out of the house without one. Your parents would have killed you."

Bif smiled and nodded affirmatively.

"Do you remember how you looked?" Susan asked him. "You always had that green knapsack on your back and wore those rumpled shorts that were patched in the back and stringy where they had been cut off. I remember you had a faded blue T-shirt and sandals. Your hair hung long and straight, and you gathered it into a knot at the back held by a triple-twisted rubber band. You had that big gold ring dangling from your ear."

Though many years had passed, they had never gotten completely out of touch. "Each person I've known," Susan had once told a friend, "is still a friend. I may have decided not to marry a guy, but that doesn't mean I still don't find him interesting, or that I wouldn't like to see him. But I find that I outgrow them after a while. I learn from each person I spend time with; then I get bored and want to move on. But it's still nice to see a person again and so I keep in touch."

Susan paused, looking at Bif. Then she asked, "Do you still go hiking in the mountains?"

"No," he answered, "it's been a long time since I've been in the West."

Susan hesitated before replying, her usually playful aspect subsiding into disappointment. She lifted her glass slowly and sipped the contents. Setting the glass down, she looked directly into her companion's eyes. "It's a good thing I didn't marry you," she said.

Bif was startled. He waited for the flash of humor that so often followed one of Susan's comments; but her eyes kept the same steady gaze. . . .

He replied uncertainly, preparing to defend himself against whatever accusation would follow. "That's a strange thing to say," he began, "that you're glad you didn't marry me. But why?"

"Your values have changed," she answered.

"What do you mean?" Bif asked. "My values haven't changed."

"You were different then," Susan answered, less challenging now than regretful. "We were both free spirits; we weren't going to let anyone dictate our lives or tell us what to be like. You introduced me to all of it. You made me see how important it was to get away; not to let work dominate my life; not to do what other people want me to do unless I thought it was right for me. You said we had to choose between being directed by others outside us, or by what we really wanted inside us; that our parents were dedicated to obligations they had had placed on them by others and that they'd do the same to us if we let them.

"You taught me to see that the significance of the nineteen-sixties was the sense of comfort and casualness which we could feel in doing things our parents didn't do at all. We received a broader base of experience than our parents did on which to build. Those years opened up our minds, made us more liberal socially, so that we could say more, do more, explore new freedoms.

"I'm still doing it," Susan continued. "I still go out into the mountains; I still get to know new people; I still see different men. But look at you now. You don't wear your ring anymore. You dress just like a banker; you don't let your wife work; you'd have children too, if your wife could have them; you drive a big car. When I asked you if you've been out to the West lately, you said you'd like to but you just don't have the time.

"You don't have time to get outdoors. You dress like a square. You talk about dollars and investments and making money all the time. I think your values have changed a lot."

Bif grew more and more agitated. "I haven't changed at all," he insisted, his voice rising with each word, and somewhat surprised at his increasing anger. "I still like to do those things. They're still important to me. I'm just busy.". . .

She answered softly, "I get so upset when I look at you. I was in awe of you because of your courage to go into the desert and to live among the Indians. That's why I'm so disappointed now. Were the things you stood for then your real values? Or were they merely pretenses to be something you aren't?"

D. Quinn Mills, *Not Like Our Parents: How the Baby Boom Generation Is Changing America*. New York: William Morrow, 1987.

Document 11: The Middle-Class Squeeze

In the early 1980s, the U.S. unemployment rate rose to record heights as the country entered a series of economic recessions. At the same time, the price of real estate began to climb as large numbers of baby boomers competed for a limited stock of housing. As author and social critic Barbara Ehrenreich writes, these problems made it more difficult for the baby boom generation to achieve the middle-class stability of their parents' generation.

Most of us are "middle-class," or so we like to believe. But there are signs that America is becoming a more divided society: over the last decade, the rich have been getting richer; the poor have been getting more numerous; and those in the middle do not appear to be doing as well as they used to. If America is "coming back," as President Reagan reassured us in the wake of the economic malaise of the early 1980s, it may be coming back in a harsh and alien form. . . .

The optimists in the debate attribute the downward shift in earnings chiefly to the baby boomers—the 78-million-member generation that began to crowd into the labor market in the 1960s and '70s, presumably driving down wages by their sheer numbers. As the boomers age, the argument goes, their incomes will rise and America will once again be a solidly middle-class society. But a recent analysis by the economists Bennett Harrison and Chris Tilly at the Massachusetts Institute of Technology and Barry Bluestone at Boston College suggests that the bulge in the labor force created by the baby boom and business-cycle effects can account for less than one-third of the increase in income inequality that has occurred since 1978.

In fact, baby boomers may find it much more difficult to make their incomes grow over time than did their parents' generation. A study by the economists Frank S. Levy and Richard C. Michel shows that, in earlier decades, men could expect their earnings to increase by about 30 percent as they aged from forty to fifty. But men who became forty in 1973 saw their earnings actually decline by 14 percent by the time they reached fifty. If this trend continues, the baby boomers, the oldest of whom are just now turning forty, will find little solace in seniority.

The fate of the baby boomers is central to the debate about America's economic future in another way, too. Contrary to the popular stereotype, the baby boomers are not all upwardly mobile, fresh-faced consumers of mesquite cuisine and exercise equipment. The baby boom is defined as those born between 1946 and 1964, and only 5 percent of them qualify as "yuppies" (young urban professional or managerial workers earning over $30,000 a year each, or $40,000 or more for a couple). Most of them, like most Americans, are "middle-class," in the limited sense that they fall somewhere near the middle of the income distribution rather than at either extreme. But they are also young, and whether they can hold on to, or achieve, middle-class status—however defined—is a test of whether the American middle class is still capable of reproducing itself from one generation to the next.

Barbara Ehrenreich, *The Worst Years of Our Lives: Irreverent Notes from a Decade of Greed.* New York: Pantheon Books, 1990.

Document 12: Family Ideals in the 1990s

The baby boomers were raised in an era of extremely low divorce rates, but the social experiments of the 1960s gave rise to a restructuring of the American family. As research psychologist Arlene Skolnick writes, although expectations have changed, contemporary families continue to strive for old-fashioned happiness and security.

After almost three decades of social upheaval and cultural civil war, there are signs that the family debate in America has entered a new stage. By the early 1990s, the polarized political climate that had prevailed for more than a decade seemed to be fading and the contours of a new consensus began to emerge. Most Americans, according to survey data and in-depth studies of attitudes, have already made peace between the liberal values of the 1960s—self fulfillment, equal opportunity for women—and the traditional work and family values of the 1980s. The most dramatic evidence of such a shift was the formation in 1991 of an unusual alliance of a group of well-known liberals and New Right conservatives; disregarding the issues that continue to divide them, such as abortion, they joined forces to press for specific family support issues on which they could agree.

Further, despite continuing talk of family decline, the outlines of a new American family are beginning to be seen. It is more diverse, more fragile, more fluid than in the past. The image of a vast, homogenized middle class that was mythologized in the 1950s applies even less to today's realities than it did then. Yet contrary to some critics, the middle class, and middle-class aspirations for family life, have not disappeared. Although there is much more tolerance for variation, lifelong heterosexual marriage, with children, remains the preferred cultural norm.

The New American Dream mixes the new cultural freedoms with many of the old wishes—marital and family happiness, economic security, home ownership, education of children. But the new dream is more demanding than the old, and even the basics— a secure job, a home, health care, education—are becoming more difficult to achieve. The new life course has more twists and turns than it did in the past; it offers greater opportunities for autonomy, but greater risks of loneliness. Further, even the middle class faces more travails than in the past: divorce, time pressures, and the dilemmas of raising children in a world that has grown more dangerous, competitive, and uncertain.

The meaning of other aspects of family change can also be debated endlessly, but the argument obscures a complex reality: the glass is both half full and half empty. It is possible to be optimistic about the future of the family and still be concerned about the number of children who live in poverty, the disruptions of divorce, the difficulties of balancing work and family.

On one issue, however—the centrality of family in the lives of most Americans—the optimists are surely correct and the pessimists wrong. For better or worse, family life, and an idealized image of what the family should be, remain at the source of our greatest joys, our deepest worries, our most painful hurts.

Arlene Skolnick, *Embattled Paradise: The American Family in the Age of Uncertainty.* New York: BasicBooks, 1991.

Document 13: The Musical Tyranny of the Boomers

The American population has continued to grow since the baby boomers came along, but those who have been born since, such as the so-called Generation X, have been unable to steal the spotlight from the boomers. As former assistant to the speaker of the U.S. House of Representatives Robert A. George writes, this reality has created intergenerational hostility between the boomers and those who have followed.

Music remains the most significant generational artifact of the Boomers. And as they have gotten older, they have held onto "their" music to a tyrannical degree (just as their public service side tends to do politically). In the 1960s and 1970s, there once was a thing called Top 40 radio, which played a mixture of musical styles: rhythm & blues, rock 'n' roll, country. The rock 'n' roll era included everybody from the Beatles to Aretha Franklin to Johnny Cash. There was something of a common musical culture, in which different styles all had a chance of being played on the same station.

Then a funny thing happened: Boomers grew up and they suddenly decided they didn't like certain kinds of "young people's music" (i.e., music made by people slightly younger than they). So they went about and made sure everything was categorized so *their* music would remain a dominant force. Thus, we got "Classic" Rock, we got Adult Contemporary, we got music divided and further subdivided. When young people in the mid- to late '70s (the early Generation X wave) moved toward disco and punk, the music was derided or ignored (and in the case of disco, ultimately Vanished from the Top 40 airwaves and sent to the ghettos of "urban radio").

In the '80s, the Boomers got around to producing that navel-contemplating, self-absorbed movie they always wanted to make (remember, it takes time to get movies done): *The Big Chill*. This, of course, produced a soundtrack that gave us a steady diet of that wonderful sixties music well into the mid-'80s. We now live in a world where every *Murphy Brown* episode opens with a sixties song. . . . Every other commercial apparently must have some 1960s tune to sell beer, cars, or whatever (at one point, during the 1997 NCAA championship game, no less than four [possibly five] consecutive commercials had a song from between 1968 and 1973 in its soundtrack). Literally, as this is being written, a 40-something farmer is driving around in his 1997 Nissan Altima, singing along to the sounds of the Monkees' "I'm a Believer." The Chambers Brothers' "Time Has Come Today," once a song chronicling youthful exuberance and the possibility of change (societal), is now the theme for Boomers putting away a financial nest egg. Boomers loved the sixties so much, they won't let them die.

And the beat goes on—appropriately enough, did I forget to mention that Sonny Bono [became] a member of Congress? The dominating cultural ethos of the Baby Boomers (this "'60s thing") is inextricably linked to their political governing mode. Woodstock was the love-in that so many of the Boomers running things now can't forget—or will let any of us forget, whether we lived it or not. Forget about the fact that many Woodstock performers died of drug overdoses; forget about the trash left in its wake; forget about the disease that is the product of their free love. For this privileged group, their memories are all peace, love, and understanding. Well, not quite: In the '90s, the elected leaders of the generation find themselves balanced somewhere between the temperaments of Woodstock and Altamont [where there were brutal beatings and one murder]. They provoke confrontation while demanding to be loved. Result: Bill Clinton (key word: "change"), Republican Congress (key word: "revolution"). Can you say "government shutdown"? I thought you could.

Richard D. Thau and Jay S. Heflin, eds., *Generations Apart: Xers vs. Boomers vs. the Elderly.* Amherst, NY: Prometheus Books, 1997.

Chronology

1945
World War II ends with the Japanese surrender in August; the U.S. population is slightly under 140 million as the postwar baby boom begins.

1946
The U.S. birthrate increases 20 percent as veterans return home from the war; only seven thousand TV sets exist in the United States; *The Common Sense Book of Child and Baby Care*, by Benjamin Spock, M.D., becomes a best-seller, ushering in an era of liberal child care.

1949
The Soviet Union conducts tests of the atom bomb, heating up the cold war arms race.

1950
Census shows 152 million people living in the United States—an increase of 12 million in the five years since the war ended; the gross national product reaches $284 million, having tripled since 1940; American families own 4.4 million televisions.

1951
Employment of women reaches peak of 19.3 million; Cleveland, Ohio, disc jockey Alan Freed begins to play rock and roll records on *The Moondog Show* on radio station WJW; J.D. Salinger publishes *Catcher in the Rye*, an anthem to teenage rebellion later embraced by millions of baby boomers.

1952
TV Guide magazine is founded; first hydrogen bomb is exploded by the United States; Republican Dwight D. Eisenhower is elected president of the United States.

1953
First hydrogen bomb is exploded by the Soviet Union.

1954
Supreme Court orders school desegregation and declares "separate but equal schools" illegal in the landmark case *Brown v. Board of Education*.

1955

Bill Haley and the Comets have number-one hit with "Rock Around the Clock"; in later months, Chuck Berry's "Maybellene" becomes a number-one hit, closely followed by Little Richard's "Tutti Frutti"; Disneyland, the world's first theme park, opens in California; McDonald's opens its first fast-food restaurants; Americans are buying TV sets at the rate of twenty thousand a day.

1956

Elvis Presley has first number-one hit with "Heartbreak Hotel."

1957

The baby boom reaches its peak as a baby is born in America every seven seconds and the population soars to almost 172 million—an increase of 32 million since the end of WWII; Jack Kerouac publishes *On the Road*, which would eventually inspire millions of baby boomers to "hit the road."

1958

Elvis Presley enters the U.S. Army; the first domestic jet-airline passenger service begins between New York City and Miami.

1959

Rock innovator Buddy Holly dies in an airplane crash near Mason City, Iowa, along with fellow musicians Richie Valens and the Big Bopper.

1960

The first sit-in by African Americans is staged at a whites-only lunch counter at a Woolworth's in Greensboro, North Carolina; John F. Kennedy is elected president; Enovid, the first birth control pill, is approved by the Food and Drug Administration for prescription; Americans own 50 million televisions, and 90 percent of American homes have at least one TV.

1961

The United States supplies the South Vietnamese army with thirty-six helicopters and four hundred American advisers, providing direct military support for the first time; the Peace Corps is founded, allowing idealistic baby boomers to travel to Third World countries to help the poor.

1962

Rachel Carson publishes *Silent Spring*, the first book about the dangers of pesticides in the environment.

1963

Martin Luther King Jr. gives his "I Have a Dream" speech during the March on Washington; President John F. Kennedy is assassinated in Dallas, Texas; Lyndon Johnson becomes president of the United States; Betty Friedan's groundbreaking book, *The Feminine Mystique*, about women's lack of equal rights, is published.

1964

Seventeen-year-olds compose the largest age group in the United States, and 24 million people are between the ages of fifteen and twenty-four; British pop music group the Beatles visits the United States for the first time and appears on television's popular *Ed Sullivan Show*; several of their songs soar to the top of the charts making them the most popular band in America; about fifteen hundred students take over campus administration buildings at the University of California at Berkeley to protest restrictions on speech; the Civil Rights Act of 1964, prohibiting discrimination on the basis of race, is passed by Congress; Timothy Leary publishes *The Psychedelic Experience*, which popularizes his experiences with LSD.

1965

The first American combat troops arrive in South Vietnam; the Watts neighborhood, an African American section of Los Angeles, erupts in a five-day riot after white police officers beat a black motorist; the first massive antiwar protests are held across the United States after American planes bomb North Vietnam.

1966

Almost 50 percent of Americans are under the age of twenty-six; the National Organization for Women (NOW) is founded by Betty Friedan and others; Huey Newton and Bobby Seale found the Black Panther Party in Oakland, California.

1967

Thousands of hippies converge on San Francisco for what later would be named the "Summer of Love"; over fifty thousand anti–Vietnam War demonstrators protest at the Lincoln Memorial in Washington, D.C.

1968

Martin Luther King Jr. is assassinated in Memphis, Tennessee; race riots erupt across America; Robert F. Kennedy is assassinated in Los Angeles after winning the California Democratic primary; the Democratic Convention is held in Chicago; when tens of thousands of antiwar protesters arrive in the city, police beat and gas them along with members of the press and convention delegates; Richard Nixon is elected president; the bloodiest year of the Vietnam War sees 14,314 Americans killed and 150,000 wounded while 500,000 U.S. troops are stationed in Indochina.

1969
Six million baby boomers admit to having taken LSD and 20 million—more than one in four—say they have smoked marijuana; the Woodstock Music and Art Fair attracts around four hundred thousand people to Bethel, New York, for three days of peace, love, and music featuring acts such as Janis Joplin, Jimi Hendrix, the Who, and the Grateful Dead.

1970
The U.S. population hits 205 million; of that 35 million Americans are between the ages of fifteen and twenty-four and there are 7 million college students in America; millions of people across the United States celebrate the first "Earth Day," signifying a beginning of the environmental movement; in an effort to expand the Vietnam War, President Richard Nixon sends thirty thousand American soldiers into neighboring Cambodia; students protest the Cambodia invasion at colleges across the country; four students are killed and nine wounded when National Guard troops open fire on demonstrators at Kent State University in Ohio; the Clean Air Act, limiting air pollution, is passed by Congress as a result of grass-roots environmental pressures.

1971
More than fifty thousand homosexuals demonstrate in favor of gay liberation in New York City's Central Park; the first video players, or VCRs, are sold.

1972
In an official study commissioned by Nixon, a blue-ribbon panel advocates decriminalization of marijuana; men working for Nixon's White House staff break into the Watergate Hotel in Washington, D.C., to place listening devices in the offices of the Democratic National Committee; discovery of these events leads to extended Congressional hearings; Nixon is reelected in a landslide victory against George McGovern, who promised to end the Vietnam War immediately; *Ms.* magazine is launched and its three hundred thousand copies sell out in only eight days while garnering an unheard-of twenty-six thousand subscription orders; the

digital age begins as more than 2.5 million Americans buy desk and pocket calculators, many of which cost over $100.

1973

The Supreme Court legalizes abortion with the *Roe v. Wade* decision; Nixon announces that a cease-fire will begin in Vietnam and the U.S. commitment in Vietnam, which began in 1954, is over; during the seven-year war, 3,330,000 mostly baby boomer Americans served in Vietnam, 58,183 were killed, 307,713 wounded; an estimated 3 million Vietnamese were killed along with hundreds of thousands in Laos and Cambodia; by May, the last U.S. combat troops in Vietnam return home; a group of oil-producing Arab states, formally OPEC, send shock waves through the U.S. economy by drastically reducing production and doubling the price of oil; in reaction to oil shortages, Nixon bans Sunday gas sales and lowers the national speed limit to 55 mph.

1974

Under threat of certain impeachment Richard Nixon becomes the only president in U.S. history to resign; Vice President Gerald Ford becomes president.

1975

The United Nations declares 1975 as the International Year of the Woman; U.S. unemployment reaches highest level since the Great Depression; baby boomer Bill Gates founds Microsoft.

1976

Democrat Jimmy Carter is elected president; Steve Wozniak sells the Apple I computer at several small retail stores for $666.66.

1977

The golden age of disco music ensues as the nightclub Studio 54 opens in New York City and the film *Saturday Night Fever* breaks box-office records; punk music reaches new heights as the Sex Pistols release "God Save the Queen" and punk fashions are featured in *Women's Wear Daily;* Elvis Presley dies of a prescription drug overdose in Memphis.

1978

For the first time in history, more women than men enroll in college; congressional inquiries into the assassination of John F. Kennedy in 1963 conclude that a conspiracy was likely, and that Lee Harvey Oswald was not solely responsible for the president's death; aging baby boomers elevate running to a national fad as 40 million Americans claim to jog at least once a week.

1979
Radioactive gases are leaked into the atmosphere as the Three Mile Island nuclear power plant in Pennsylvania is threatened with meltdown; sixty-five thousand antinuclear activists protest in Washington, D.C.; oil shortages create lines around gas stations and California is forced to institute rationing, and OPEC raises prices another 24 percent; bank interest rates soar, putting the dream of home ownership out of reach for millions of baby boomers; extremist Iranian students seize U.S. embassy in Tehran and take 52 Americans hostage.

1980
Seventy percent of baby boomers interviewed in a national poll said they wished they had gone to Woodstock; Ronald Reagan becomes the fortieth president of the United States in a landslide victory over incumbent Jimmy Carter.

1981
President Reagan is shot and wounded in Washington, D.C., by young gunman John Hinckley; Sandra Day O'Connor is unanimously approved by the Senate to become the first female U.S. Supreme Court justice; personal computers introduced by IBM.

1982
Tens of thousands of people march in New York City against Reagan arms buildup in the largest protest against nuclear weapons in history; the Equal Rights Amendment, which would have outlawed discrimination against women, is defeated after a ten-year fight for ratification; the United States records an unemployment rate of 10.4 percent, the highest since 1940.

1984
The first Macintosh computer is released with 128K RAM, selling for almost $2,500; the Vietnam War Memorial is unveiled in Washington, D.C.

1985
The Live Aid concert is held simultaneously in London and Philadelphia, raising $70 million for starving people in Africa; Reagan meets with Soviet premier Mikhail Gorbachev in Geneva, Switzerland, for the first superpower summit of the decade.

1986
Martin Luther King Day is made an official national holiday; the space shuttle *Challenger* explodes just moments after liftoff; the public learns that the United States has sent spare parts and ammunition to Iran, touching off the Iran-Contra scandal.

1987
Iran-Contra hearings are held before House and Senate committees; Reagan and George Bush continue to deny knowledge, while Oliver North is assigned much of the blame for the illegal activities.

1988
George Bush is elected the forty-first president; his vice president is Dan Quayle.

1989
The supertanker *Exxon Valdez* hits a reef in Prince William Sound, Alaska, and dumps 1 million gallons of crude oil over a sixteen-hundred-square-mile area, contaminating more than eight hundred miles of shoreline; the Berlin Wall is pulled down in Germany, signaling the end of Soviet rule in Eastern Europe.

1990
Iraqi forces invade Kuwait, sending U.S. gas prices soaring.

1991
Coalition airplanes begin massive bombing raids on Iraq to begin Operation Desert Storm; the ensuing Gulf War ends in just over a month; the Soviet legislature suspends all activities of the Communist Party; for the first time in seventy years, the USSR is not ruled by Communists.

1992
Not-guilty verdict in the Rodney King police brutality case ignites riots in Los Angeles; Bill Clinton and Al Gore win the national presidential race.

1993
Janet Reno is appointed as the first female attorney general of the United States; the Internet comes into widespread use.

1994
Three hundred fifty Republican candidates gather on the steps of the Capitol building to sign the Contract with America; in midterm elections, Republicans gain a majority in the House and Senate for the first time in over forty years.

1995
The Alfred P. Murrah Building in Oklahoma City is bombed, killing 168. At the time it was the most destructive terrorist act on American soil.

1997
President Bill Clinton announces a plan to link every U.S. classroom to the Internet by the year 2000; researchers in Scotland clone a lamb named Dolly from a single cell of an adult sheep; the Congressional Budget Office releases a report stating that retiring baby boomers will put such a strain on Social Security, Medicare, and other government programs by 2020 that the entire U.S. economy will be threatened.

1998
The drug Viagra is introduced to help aging male baby boomers improve sexual performance; House Judiciary Committee approves two articles of impeachment against President Clinton, charging him with lying to a grand jury and obstructing justice by covering up his affair with White House aide Monica Lewinsky.

1999
The Senate votes 55 to 45 against convicting Clinton of perjury, and 50-50 on the obstruction of justice charge; the vote puts an end to the possibility of Clinton's impeachment.

2000
The first wave of baby boomers turns fifty-five.

2001
U.S. population is more than 284 million—an increase of 144 million since the end of World War II.

For Further Research

Terry H. Anderson, *The Movement and the Sixties*. New York: Oxford University Press, 1995.

Anthony M. Casale and Philip Lerman, *Where Have All the Flowers Gone? The Fall and Rise of the Woodstock Generation*. Kansas City, MO: Andrews and McMeel, 1989.

Eldridge Cleaver, *Soul on Ice*. New York: Dell, 1968.

Andrew J. Edelstein and Kevin McDonough, *The Seventies from Hot Pants to Hot Tubs*. New York: Dutton, 1990.

Barbara Ehrenreich, *The Worst Years of Our Lives: Irreverent Notes from a Decade of Greed*. New York: Pantheon, 1990.

Joe Eszterhas, *American Rhapsody*. New York: Knopf, 2000.

Sara M. Evans, *Born for Liberty: A History of Women in America*. New York: Free Press, 1989.

David Farber, *The Great Age of Dreams: America in the 1960s*. New York: Hill and Wang, 1994.

Edgar Z. Friedenberg, ed., *The Anti-American Generation*. New Brunswick, NJ: Transaction, 1972.

David Frum, *How We Got Here*. New York: Basic Books, 2000.

Holly George-Warren, ed., *The Rolling Stone Book of the Beats*. New York: Hyperion, 1999.

Todd Gitlin, *The Sixties: Years of Hope, Days of Rage*. New York: Bantam, 1987.

Michael Gross, *My Generation*. New York: HarperCollins, 2000.

David Halberstam, *The Fifties*. New York: Villard, 1993.

Brett Harvey, *The Fifties: A Women's Oral History*. New York: HarperCollins, 1993.

Barney Hoskyns, *Beneath the Diamond Sky: Haight-Ashbury 1965–1970*. New York: Simon & Schuster, 1997.

Gerald Howard, ed., *The Sixties: Art, Politics, and Media of Our Most Explosive Decade*. New York: Paragon House, 1991.

Landon Y. Jones, *Great Expectations: America and the Baby Boom Generation*. New York: Coward, McCann & Geoghegan, 1980.

Kenneth Keniston, *Young Radicals: Notes on Committed Youth.* New York: Harcourt, Brace & World, 1968.

Timothy Leary, *The Politics of Ecstasy.* Berkeley, CA: Ronin, 1998.

Martin A. Lee and Bruce Shlain, *Acid Dreams.* New York: Grove Weidenfeld, 1992.

Nina C. Leibman, *Living Room Lectures: The Fifties Family in Film and Television.* Austin: University of Texas Press, 1995.

Suzanne Levine and Harriet Lyons, eds., *The Decade of Women.* New York: G.P. Putnam's Sons, 1980.

Paul C. Light, *Baby Boomers.* New York: W.W. Norton, 1988.

Marci McDonald, "New Designs for Aging Hipsters," *U.S. News & World Report,* April 2, 2001.

Douglas T. Miller and Marion Nowak, *The Fifties: The Way We Really Were.* Garden City, NY: Doubleday, 1975.

Timothy Miller, *The Hippies and American Values.* Knoxville: University of Tennessee Press, 1991.

D. Quinn Mills, *Not Like Our Parents: How the Baby Boom Generation Is Changing America.* New York: William Morrow, 1987.

Aldon D. Morris, *The Origins of the Civil Rights Movement.* New York: Free Press, 1984.

Lynda Rosen Obst, ed., *The Sixties: The Decade Remembered Now by the People Who Lived Then.* New York: Rolling Stone Press, 1977.

Daniel Okrent, "Twilight of the Boomers," *Time,* June 12, 2000.

John Parikhal, *The Baby Boom: Making Sense of Our Generation at Forty.* Ontario, Canada: Joint Communications Corporation, 1993.

Bruce Pollock, *Hipper than Our Kids.* New York: Schirmer, 1993.

Gilbert T. Sewall, ed., *The Eighties: A Reader.* Reading, MA: Addison-Wesley, 1997.

Philip Shabecoff, *A Fierce Green Fire.* New York: Hill and Wang, 1993.

Tom Shachtman, *Decade of Shocks: Dallas to Watergate, 1963–1974.* New York: Poseidon Press, 1983.

Arlene Skolnick, *Embattled Paradise: The American Family in the Age of Uncertainty.* New York: BasicBooks, 1991.

Arthur Stein, *Seeds of the Seventies*. Hanover, NH: University Press of New England, 1985.

William Sterling and Stephen White, *Boomernomics*. New York: Library of Contemporary Thought, 1998.

Jane and Michael Stern, *Encyclopedia of Pop Culture*. New York: HarperPerennial, 1987.

———, *Sixties People*. New York: Knopf, 1990.

Terry Teachout, ed., *Beyond the Boom: New Voices on American Life, Culture, and Politics*. New York: Poseidon Press, 1990.

Richard D. Thau and Jay S. Heflin, eds., *Generations Apart: Xers vs. Boomers vs. the Elderly*. Amherst, NY: Prometheus, 1997.

Irwin Unger and Debi Unger, eds., *The Times Were a Changin': The Sixties Reader*. New York: Three Rivers Press, 1998.

Ed Ward, *Rock of Ages: The* Rolling Stone *History of Rock & Roll*. New York: Rolling Stone Press, 1986.

Index